Early Praise for *Text Processing with JavaScript*

There's nothing *regular* about working with regular expressions. Turn the mundane yet tedious task of processing textual data into a manageable and even a fun experience using the techniques and recipes in this book.

➤ **Dr. Venkat Subramaniam**
Award-winning author and founder of Agile Developer, Inc

While it would be easy for a book like *Text Processing with JavaScript* to spend all of its time on regular expressions, here you'll also find ample discussion and useful examples of humble, often-overlooked, and computationally less expensive string methods in JavaScript. Whatever your text-processing task, this book will point you to the right API for the job. And even readers who might not be doing heavy-duty text processing will benefit from the coverage here of multi-byte character sets and presentations of various non-Western-Latin alphabets, including emoji, which is a tremendously useful resource in its own right.

➤ **Karl Stolley**
Web developer and author of *Programming WebRTC*

A wealth of JavaScript tips, tricks, and tools, *Text Processing with JavaScript* is loaded with recipes ranging from password validation to internationalization to simply working with formatted numbers. Faraz shows you the built-in functions you can use to tackle your JS problems, then expands to regular expressions for any complex situations you may face.

➤ **Michael Fazio**
Engineering Manager at Albert and author of *Kotlin and Android Development featuring Jetpack*

A handful of domain-specific languages exist that richly reward the software developers who master them. For DevOps engineers, the key DSL is bash; for backend engineers, it's SQL; and for frontend and full-stack engineers, it's regular expressions. Expertly wielding any of these languages is a superpower. *Text Processing with JavaScript* showcases how to harness the power of the JavaScript string type, diving deeply into all its aspects. Even developers with years of JavaScript experience will discover something new in its pages. With detailed coverage of various native text processing APIs, meticulous examples of regular expression techniques, and insightful code explanations, this book deserves a place on every frontend developer's bookshelf.

➤ **Matt Frisbie**
    Author of *Professional JavaScript for Web Developers*

This book helps readers master text processing through its comprehensive knowledge, abundant real-world examples, and detailed explanations. I'd recommend it to anyone who wants to learn and delve deeper into *Text Processing with JavaScript*.

➤ **Bowen**
    The creator of *Regex Vis*

Text Processing with JavaScript

Regular Expressions, Tools, and Techniques for Optimal Performance

Faraz K. Kelhini

The Pragmatic Bookshelf

Dallas, Texas

When we are aware that a term used in this book is claimed as a trademark, the designation is printed with an initial capital letter or in all capitals.

The Pragmatic Starter Kit, The Pragmatic Programmer, Pragmatic Programming, Pragmatic Bookshelf, PragProg and the linking g device are trademarks of The Pragmatic Programmers, LLC.

Every precaution was taken in the preparation of this book. However, the publisher assumes no responsibility for errors or omissions, or for damages that may result from the use of information (including program listings) contained herein.

For our complete catalog of hands-on, practical, and Pragmatic content for software developers, please visit *https://pragprog.com*.

The team that produced this book includes:

Publisher:	Dave Thomas
COO:	Janet Furlow
Managing Editor:	Tammy Coron
Development Editor:	Margaret Eldridge
Copy Editor:	Vanya Wryter
Indexing:	Potomac Indexing, LLC
Layout:	Gilson Graphics

For sales, volume licensing, and support, please contact *support@pragprog.com*.

For international rights, please contact *rights@pragprog.com*.

ISBN-13: 979-8-88865-033-2
Book version: P1.0—December 2023

Contents

Acknowledgments

Writing a programming book is a collaborative effort that would not have been possible without the support and expertise of many individuals.

I extend my sincere appreciation to the team at The Pragmatic Programmers, who believed in the potential of this book and provided invaluable guidance and resources. Their editorial team and design professionals have played a pivotal role in shaping the content of this work. In particular, I would like to thank my editor, Margaret Eldridge, whose meticulous attention to detail was instrumental in identifying and rectifying gaps in my writing.

A big thanks to experts who reviewed the book prior to publication, including Michael Fazio, Karl Stolley, Andy Lester, Trevor Burnham, and Jason Montojo. These wonderful developers offered very helpful insight into the code quality and ensured that this book met the highest standards of accuracy and clarity.

Thank you, also, to Dr. Venkat Subramaniam, Matt Frisbie, and Bowen who were kind enough to offer words of encouragement and praise for the book.

To my readers, thank you for choosing this book as your learning companion. Your enthusiasm for learning and your curiosity motivate me to continue exploring and sharing knowledge.

To everyone who contributed directly or indirectly to this project, thank you all for being a part of this project. Your support and contributions have made this endeavor truly rewarding.

Faraz K. Kelhini

Preface

Most popular programming languages support regular expressions, and there's a good reason for that: regular expressions are incredibly powerful at text processing. With regular expressions, you can greatly reduce the time and effort required for complex string parsing tasks that would otherwise take dozens of lines of code.

But, as a JavaScript developer, you may not need to jump into writing regular expression patterns whenever you need to process texts. JavaScript already provides excellent built-in tools that meet many of your text manipulation needs.

In this book, you'll explore when and how to use each tool by working through real-world scenarios. You'll learn the mechanics of JavaScript's regex in detail via cookbook-style recipes for various text manipulation tasks.

Make sure you actually type and execute the code examples as you follow along in the book. Some examples may appear simple, but there's a big difference between reading the code and being able to write it on your own.

Who Is This Book For?

This book is geared toward the needs of both client- and server-side programmers. Whether you're a beginner or an advanced programmer, this guide will save you a ton of time when dealing with textual data. We'll focus squarely on the practical aspects of text processing with JavaScript—that is, what each technique is designed to accomplish and how to use it in your program.

Readers who have experience with regular expressions will still benefit from this book as it contains a wealth of detail on JavaScript's regular expression flavor as well as features recently introduced. By the end of this book, you will be able to solve a great many complex validation, modification, and search-and-replace problems rapidly and efficiently.

What You Should Know

To use this book, you should already know basic JavaScript, HTML, and CSS syntax. Use of HTML and CSS will be infrequent and fairly basic, and I'll explain each JavaScript example in detail. So even if your knowledge is rusty, you'll understand how the code works.

To run the examples, you'll need a JavaScript environment that supports the newest version of the ECMAScript standard (ECMAScript is the official standard that defines the specification of JavaScript). So, whether you're running the examples in your browser's console or the Node.js environment, make sure you have the latest software version installed.

Certain recipes use APIs that are only available in the browser environment, such as fetch(). As a result, you can run those recipes only in a browser. We'll warn you about the lack of browser/environment support whenever necessary.

What's in This Book?

We've organized the book as a cookbook, so you can quickly jump to different recipes. But if you read the book cover to cover, you'll become a master chef of text processing. There are three primary parts in this book:

- Part 1 contains recipes that solve various text processing problems with JavaScript's built-in methods.

- Part 2 covers JavaScript's flavor of regex, provides an in-depth discussion of the syntax, and gives various examples of using them.

- Part 3 provides solutions to a wide range of retrieval and alteration tasks. These recipes will give you the helping hand you need to become a regular expression expert.

Online Resources

To download the example code used in the book, please visit the Pragmatic Bookshelf website.[1] You can submit feedback and errata entries, get up-to-date information, and join in the discussions on the book's forum page. If you're reading the book in PDF format, you can view or download a specific example by clicking on the little gray box above the code.

---

1.   https://pragprog.com/titles/fkjavascript/text-processing-with-javascript/#resources

CHAPTER 1

Part I: Text Processing with Built-in JavaScript Methods

Many regard regular expressions as the holy grail of text processing—a tool that can simplify numerous programming tasks and provide a compact, effective solution to various text processing problems. But should you shoe-horn regular expressions into situations where standard built-in solutions already exist?

Of course not. Regular expressions can be tricky to get right, and it's too easy to end up with a pattern that accepts more input than intended. Code collaboration may also become an issue, as the cryptic nature of regular expressions may discourage your fellow programmers from reviewing or debugging your code. After all, nobody wants to spend a week trying to understand a twenty-line enigmatic string made of magical symbols.

In part one of the book, we'll delve into a collection of tiny programs demonstrating built-in string manipulation methods in JavaScript. You'll discover what problems each method is designed to solve, and in doing so, you'll learn in what situations they're preferable to regular expressions.

Recipe 1

Determining If a Value Is a String with the typeof Operator

Task

In Javascript, you will often need to validate that a value is a string. For example, in the next recipe, we'll build a function that searches for multiple words in a string. Before you pass a value to the function, you'd want to check if it's a string. Any other data type, like a number or Boolean, would cause your function to throw an error.

Throughout this book, you will see functions of this sort repeatedly, so it's a good place to start.

Solution

Use the typeof operator:

```
part_1/determining_valid_strings/typeof_ex1.js
function isString(value) {
  return typeof value === "string";
}

isString(123);      // → false
isString("abc");    // → true
```

The typeof operator returns a string indicating a value's type.

Discussion

In JavaScript, you can create a string literal with single or double quotes or the backticks:

```
part_1/determining_valid_strings/typeof_ex2.js
let str1 = "string";
let str2 = 'string';
let str3 = `string`;
```

So, a number enclosed in quotation marks or backticks is not a number anymore but a string. You can also create a string with the String() constructor if you call it without the new keyword:

```
part_1/determining_valid_strings/typeof_ex3.js
String(123);     // → "123"
```

In a string, each character occupies a position. Index 0 corresponds to the first character, index 1 to the second character, and so on. So, to get the second character in a string, you can type str[1]:

```
part_1/determining_valid_strings/typeof_ex4.js
let str = "string";

console.log(str[1]);    // → t
```

Up next, we'll begin our journey into the realm of JavaScript text processing methods by building a function that checks whether a string contains a list of words.

Recipe 2

Checking a String for Specific Words with includes()

Task

Suppose you're building an online bakeshop and want to filter messages so they can be routed to the correct baker. You need to check the strings in incoming emails to account for different spellings of words like "doughnut" versus "donut." You can't use the includes() method alone because it allows you to look for only a single word.

Solution

Put the words you want to search for in an array. Then create a function that accepts two arguments: a string to search and an array of words. Inside the function, search for each word in the string and return true if at least one search is successful:

```
part_1/checking_specific_words/includes_ex1.js
const msg = "I'd like to order two donuts";
const words = ["doughnut", "donut"];

function hasSomeWords(str, arr) {
  return arr.some(el => str.includes(el));
}

hasSomeWords(msg, words);    // → true
```

The some() method returns true if at least one element in the array passes the test implemented by the given function. In this case, that means includes() first searches for "doughnut." Since there's no such a word in the string, the method returns false. The second time includes() searches for "donut," and this time it returns true. So, the return value of some() will be true.

Discussion

ECMAScript added includes() to the language in ES2015 to enable developers to easily determine whether a string contains another string. The second argument of includes() is optional and lets you specify the position at which to begin searching. For example:

part_1/checking_specific_words/includes_ex2.js
```
const quote = "Sachertorte is a torte of Austrian origin.";

quote.includes("Sachertorte", 15);    // → false
```

This code starts the search at index 15. Because no word matches "Sachertorte" from index 15 onwards, the return value is false.

Remember, includes() is case sensitive. If you search for "Sachertorte" in a string containing "SacherTorte," the result is false:

part_1/checking_specific_words/includes_ex3.js
```
const quote = "I'd like to order a SacherTorte.";
const word = "Sachertorte";

quote.includes(word);    // → false
```

Some desserts could have internal capitalization because they are made up of two words such as Dobostorta/DobosTorta, Leibnizkeks/LeibnizKeks, and SacherTorte/Sachertorte. So, in most cases, you want to perform a case-insensitive search by converting both the string and the keyword to lowercase, like this:

part_1/checking_specific_words/includes_ex4.js
```
const quote = "I'd like to order a SacherTorte.".toLowerCase();
const word = "Sachertorte".toLowerCase();

quote.includes(word);    // → true
```

But what if you want to check if a string contains multiple words simultaneously? In that case, you should use the every() method. every() is similar to some() in that it executes a function for each element of an array. But it returns true only if every item in the array passes the test. Here's an example:

```
part_1/checking_specific_words/includes_ex5.js
const msg = "1 sachertorte, 3 pretzels, and 2 donuts please.";
const wordsArr1 = ["sachertorte", "donut"];
const wordsArr2 = ["sachertorte", "sourdough"];

function hasEveryWord(str, arr) {
  return arr.every(el => str.includes(el));
}

hasEveryWord(msg, wordsArr1);    // → true
hasEveryWord(msg, wordsArr2);    // → false
```

Here, "sachertorte" and "donut" pass the test because they both exist in the string, but that's not the case for "sachertorte" and "sourdough."

Although includes() is designed to search for only a single word, with a little effort, you can take advantage of it to search for more words. But be careful when looking for words that also have a compound form.

If you search for "cake" in "I'd like to order two pancakes," includes() returns true. If you don't want that to happen, you should use a regex token known as a word boundary. See Recipe 25, Looking For Whole Words Only with the Word Boundary (\b), on page 67.

Recipe 3

Matching the Beginning or End of a String with startsWith() and endsWith()

Task

Let's assume you have a database of articles about pet care and your task is to compile a list of questions that are answered in the articles. Suppose the articles are formatted in the Markdown language and the questions are all in level 2 heading tags (preceded with ##).

How would you write a code that distinguishes a heading from a normal sentence? And what would you use if you wanted to filter those that are questions? You need a solution that lets you check the characters at the beginning and end of a string.

Solution

First, we'll use the startsWith() method to determine if the string begins with ##:

```js
const str1 = "## Why is chocolate bad for your dog?";
const str2 = "# 10 Amazing Dog Facts";
const searchStr = "##";

str1.startsWith(searchStr);    // → true
str2.startsWith(searchStr);    // → false
```

Then we'll use the endsWith() method to check if the string ends with a question mark:

```js
const str1 = "## Why is chocolate bad for your dog?";
const str2 = "## Best way to trim your dog's nails";
const searchStr = "?";

str1.endsWith(searchStr);    // → true
str2.endsWith(searchStr);    // → false
```

Now that we know startsWith() and endsWith() produce the result we want, let's create a function that performs both these operations at the same time:

```js
function startsWithEndsWith(str, start, end) {
  if ((str.startsWith(start) === true) && (str.endsWith(end) === true)) {
    return true;
  } else {
    return false;
  }
}
```

We can also simplify the function by removing the if statement. The logical AND (&&) operator returns true if both startsWith() and endsWith() return true, so we can get the same result in a single statement:

```js
function startsWithEndsWith(str, start, end) {
  return str.startsWith(start) && str.endsWith(end);
}
```

This code works fine for testing a string containing a single sentence, but we want to extract level 2 Markdown headings from an article. So, we need a way to pass each line of the article to our function. Divide the string at line breaks by calling split("\n"), then loop over the resulting array with forEach() and pass each line to startsWithEndsWith():

```
part_1/matching_with_startsWith_endsWith/startsWith_endsWith_ex5.js
const str =
`## Why is chocolate bad for your dog?
Some text ...
## Best way to trim your dog's nails
More text ...
## Are there human foods that are safe for dogs?
...`;

function startsWithEndsWith(str, start, end) {
  return str.startsWith(start) && str.endsWith(end);
}

str.split("\n").forEach(str => {
  if (startsWithEndsWith(str, "##", "?")) {
    console.log(str);
  };
});

// logs:
// → ## Why is chocolate bad for your dog?
// → ## Are there human foods that are safe for dogs?
```

Success!

Browser Compatibility

 Safari 15.4, released on March 15, 2022, joined the party a little later than other leading browsers, as it incorporated at() after its major competitors had already done so. For backward compatibility with older browser versions, you need to use a polyfill.[1] In the Node environment, you'll need a minimum Node version of 16.6.0.[2]

Discussion

In JavaScript, there are often multiple ways to complete a task. As a programmer, you should usually strive to use the most efficient tool for the job. But you should also take into account the reliability and readability of your code, which are more important in most projects.

An alternative way to get the last character of a string is to use the at() method. It's compact and fast! But browser support isn't quite there yet, so you might find your code broken in older browsers.

With at(), you can retrieve a single character at a position in a string like this:

---

1. https://github.com/tc39/proposal-relative-indexing-method#polyfill
2. https://mzl.la/3FKyJMr

```
part_1/matching_with_startsWith_endsWith/startsWith_endsWith_ex6.js
const str = "Do dogs dream?";

str.at(-1);    // → "?"
str.at(-2);    // → "m"
```

When calling at() with a negative number, the method counts back from the end of the string. So, -1 gets you the last character, -2 gets you the second to last character, and so on.

Calling at() on Arrays

You can also use at() with JavaScript arrays. Check out my article on Medium to learn more.[3]

While startsWith() lets you check characters at a string's beginning, endsWith() lets you determine if a string ends with specific characters. If you want to get the value of only a single character, then at() is a compact alternative you may use, but be sure to check browser support.

Recipe 4

Extracting Lists from Text with slice()

Task

Suppose you run an online shop selling thousands of different clothes. You're tasked with making the products searchable by color. The problem is the available colors for each product are listed as a sentence in the product description. You need a way to find and extract those colors programmatically to build a searchable database.

So if you have a product description like this:

```
Feel confident in even the most unforeseen weather conditions with these
waterproof trail-running shoes helping you stay dry. Available in four new
colors: Velvet Brown, Black, Golden Moss, Medium Blue.
```

You want to extract the colors and store them in an array like this:

```
["Velvet Brown", "Black", "Golden Moss", "Medium Blue"]
```

---

3.   https://medium.com/pragmatic-programmers/at-method-in-javascript-54544ec93ccc

The list you want to extract may also come in different variations. It could have a forward slash (/) between items rather than a comma. Or it could have extra words such as "and," "or," "etc." that you don't want to end up in your array.

In this recipe, we first build a function that extracts simple lists and then enhance the function to handle more complex lists.

Solution

This recipe involves two steps: first, finding the sentence containing the list of colors, and second, extracting each color and storing it in an array. You can perform the first step using the indexOf() method. The list of colors comes after a colon (:). Locate it with indexOf() and store the resulting index in a constant. Next, locate the first period that follows the colon and store the index in another constant:

```
const str = `Feel confident in even the most unforeseen weather conditions
  with these waterproof trail-running shoes helping you stay dry. Available
  in four new colors: Velvet Brown, Black, Golden Moss, Medium Blue.`;

const start = str.indexOf(":");
const end = str.indexOf(".", start);
```

Now, you have two indexes that mark the beginning and end of the list in the string. Pass them to the slice() method to extract the list:

```
const list = str.slice(start + 2, end);
// "Velvet Brown, Black, Golden Moss, Medium Blue"
```

The arguments you pass to slice() specify the string's start and end index to be returned. To offset the colon and the space at the beginning of the string, increase the start index by 2. The end index tells slice() to extract up to but not including the character at that index, so there's no need to subtract from it.

Now comes the second step, where you need to convert the comma-separated list into an array. There are a couple of ways to do this in JavaScript. The long approach is to look for commas in a loop and add each item to an array. The more straightforward approach is to use the split() method. With split(), you can define where each split in a string should occur and quickly get an array of items:

```
const colors = list.split(", ");

console.log(colors);
// → [ "Velvet Brown", "Black", "Golden Moss", "Medium Blue" ]
```

In this code, you're telling split() to use a comma followed by a space as a separator. The result is an array of colors with no extra space or commas to worry about.

Here's the final code put together in a function so you can reuse it:

part_1/extracting_lists/slice_ex1.js
```
const str = `Feel confident in even the most unforeseen weather conditions
 with these waterproof trail-running shoes helping you stay dry. Available
 in four new colors: Velvet Brown, Black, Golden Moss, Medium Blue.`;

function extractList(str) {
  const start = str.indexOf(":");
  const end = str.indexOf(".", start);
  const list = str.slice(start + 2, end);

  return list.split(", ");
}

extractList(str);
// → [ "Velvet Brown", "Black", "Golden Moss", "Medium Blue" ]
```

Discussion

If the list you want to extract has extra words, such as "and," "or," "etc.," or uses a forward slash (/) rather than a comma, then you need a more advanced function. You probably won't find "etc." in a list of available color options for a product, but we have included it here so that you can remove it from other types of lists, if needed.

Consider this example:

part_1/extracting_lists/slice_ex2.js
```
function extractList(str) {
  const start = str.indexOf(":");
  const end = str.indexOf(".", start);
  const list = str.slice(start + 2, end);

  return list.split(", ");
}

extractList("Available in three colors: red, black, and blue.");
// → [ "red", "black", "and blue" ]

extractList("Available colors: Red/Black/Blue.");
// → "Red/Black/Blue"

extractList("Available colors: Red, Black, Blue, etc.");
// → [ "Red", "Black", "Blue", "etc" ]
```

This function isn't equipped to handle such lists properly. Let's revise it! You first need to check whether the list has a comma or a forward slash:

```
list.includes(",") ? list.split(", ") : list.split('/');
```

The includes() method checks if the list contains a comma. If so, it returns true, and the ternary operator executes list.split(", "). If not, the operator executes list.split("/").

Next, remove "etc" from the resulting array:

```
arr.at(-1) === "etc" ? arr.pop() : null;
```

at(-1) gets the last item in the array. If it has a value of "etc," pop() removes it. You could use a filter() here, but since "etc" is usually the last item in the array, it's more efficient to check only the last item's value.

Browser Compatibility

Older browsers do not support the at() method. To ensure your app can be accessed by users with older browsers, you should use a polyfill.[4] In the Node environment, you'll need a minimum Node version of 16.6.0.[5]

To remove "and"/"or," you can use map(), like this:

```
return arr.map(word => {
  if (word.startsWith("and ")) {
    return word.slice(4);
  } else if (word.startsWith("or ")) {
    return word.slice(3);
  } else {
    return word;
  }
});
```

When you call map(), it executes a function on every element in the array. Use the startsWith() method to check if there's an extra "and" or "or" at the beginning of an item and remove it with slice().

Your revised function should look like this:

```
part_1/extracting_lists/slice_ex3.js
function extractList(str) {
  const start = str.indexOf(":");
  const end = str.indexOf(".", start);
  const list = str.slice(start + 2, end);

  // Split the string by comma or forward slash
  const arr = list.includes(",") ? list.split(", ") : list.split("/");
```

---

4.   https://github.com/tc39/proposal-relative-indexing-method#polyfill

5.   https://mzl.la/3FKyJMr

```
  // Remove "etc"
  arr.at(-1) === "etc" ? arr.pop() : null;

  // Remove and/or
  return arr.map(word => {
    if (word.startsWith("and ")) {
      return word.slice(4);
    } else if (word.startsWith("or ")) {
      return word.slice(3);
    } else {
      return word;
    }
  });
}

extractList("Available in three colors: red, black, and blue.");
// → [ "Red", "Black", "Blue" ]

extractList("Available colors: Red/Black/Blue.");
// → [ "Red", "Black", "Blue" ]

extractList("Available colors: Red, Black, Blue, etc.");
// → [ "Red", "Black", "Blue" ]
```

You might be wondering why not use replaceAll() to remove any "and," "or," "etc." from the text before splitting it into an array. It's because there could be a color name containing these letters, such as "Macaroni and Cheese" (yes, that's a color name).

Take advantage of the slice() method to extract a section of a string or an array. The second argument is optional: omit it to get the rest of the string. Use split() when you need to divide a string into an array of substrings, and finally, use map() to weed out any unwanted part of the resulting array.

Recipe 5

Converting Color Names to Hexadecimal Values with the Canvas Element

Task

Suppose you're working on a drawing application that works with hexadecimal (hex) color codes. You want to provide a field that lets users enter a color name to be converted to its hex equivalence automatically.

You need a solution for converting colors into their hex representation.

Solution

Create a temporary HTML canvas element, obtain its 2D context, and use the fillStyle property to convert the color:

```
part_1/converting_color_to_hex/color_to_hex_ex1.js
function convertColorToHex(color) {
  const canvas = document.createElement("canvas");
  const ctx = canvas.getContext("2d");
  ctx.fillStyle = color;
  return ctx.fillStyle.toUpperCase();
}

convertColorToHex("Khaki");    // → "#F0E68C"
```

This function accepts a string containing a web color name and converts it into its corresponding hex value.

Discussion

Hexadecimal notation is commonly used to specify colors in programs and web development because it provides a compact and efficient way to represent a wide range of colors.

In hex notation, colors are made of a combination of red, green, and blue (RGB) values, each represented by a two-digit hex number (00 to FF), with the first two digits representing the intensity of red, the next two digits representing the intensity of green, and the last two digits representing the intensity of blue. For example, the color white is represented by the hex code #FFFFFF, which has maximum values for all three colors.

In this solution, we define a function that takes in a single parameter called color, which should be a string representing a color. Inside the function, we create a new HTML canvas element by using the document.createElement() method. This method creates an HTML element based on the tag name provided as the argument. In this case, we use the tag name "canvas" to create a canvas element.

Next, we create a context object for the canvas using the getContext() method. We specify that the context object should be for a two-dimensional canvas by passing "2d" as an argument. We then set the fillStyle property of the context object to the parameter that was passed to the function. This sets the color that will be used to fill any shapes drawn on the canvas.

Now we can read the fillStyle property of the context object to get the hex value of the color. When we call the function with the argument Khaki, it will create a canvas element, set the fillStyle to Khaki, and return the hex value of the color #F0E68C. Note that this function does not actually draw anything on the canvas—it only creates the canvas element and sets the fillStyle.

Before returning the hex value from the function, we used the toUpperCase() method to convert the hex letters to uppercase. In JavaScript and CSS, hex colors can be written using either uppercase or lowercase letters. Both uppercase and lowercase hex letters represent the same values.

But, it's common practice to use uppercase letters for hex colors because it can make the code easier to read and differentiate from other text in the code. Ultimately, the choice between the two styles is a matter of personal preference or style guide.

By converting color names to hex notation, we can specify a color in a way that can be used across different software platforms and devices. A list of web colors and their hex equivalent is available on Wikipedia.[6]

Recipe 6

Adding Transparency to Hex Colors

Task

Suppose you want to add a semi-transparent overlay to some elements of your app. For example, you may have a prompt that asks the reader to log in before proceeding, and you may want to include a semi-transparent white color around the prompt to blur the remainder of the page.

If you use a normal hexadecimal color, the overlay will completely obscure the content underneath it. If you use the CSS opacity, it will set the opacity of the element as a whole, including its contents.

You need a solution that lets you add transparency to a hex color.

---

6.   https://en.wikipedia.org/wiki/Web_colors

Solution

Write a function that accepts a hex value and a percentage as input parameters. The function should convert the percentage into a hex value and then add it to the original hex value:

part_1/adding_transparency_to_hex/adding_transparency_to_hex_ex1.js

```
function addAlphaToHex(hex, percent) {
  const decimal = percent / 100;
  const rgb = Math.round(decimal * 255);
  const alpha = rgb.toString(16).toUpperCase();

  if (alpha.length === 1) {
    alpha = "0" + alpha;
  }

  return hex + alpha;
}
addAlphaToHex("#FFFFFF", 70);    // → "#FFFFFFB3"
```

This function returns an eight-character hex value that includes the alpha level. In this case, the return value is a white hex color (#FFFFFF) with 70 percent opacity (#FFFFFFB3).

Discussion

Previously, developers had to convert a hex color to either an RGBA or HSLA color value to set opacity. This conversion was necessary because the alpha channel in the RGBA or HSLA value could be used to determine the level of opacity. However, with the introduction of CSS Color Module Level 4, the problem has been solved by adding new four (#rgba) and eight (#rrggbbaa) character hex notations that include the alpha level. So, developers no longer need to convert the hex color to another format in order to set opacity.

The rr, gg, bb, and aa in the notation represent the hexadecimal values for the red, green, blue, and alpha components respectively, ranging from 00 to FF. The alpha value determines the opacity of the color, with 00 representing a fully transparent color and FF representing a fully opaque color. For example, the color #FF0000FF is a fully opaque red color, while the color #FF000000 is a fully transparent red color.

Our function addAlphaToHex() takes two parameters: hex and percent. The function's purpose is to convert the percentage value to its corresponding hex representation and append it as an alpha value to the given hex. Within the function, we first calculate the decimal value of the percentage by dividing it by 100. Then we multiply the resulting decimal by 255 and round the result using Math.round() to obtain an RGB value.

Next, we convert the RGB value to a hexadecimal string using the toString() method with a radix of 16 (that is, base 16). We then convert the string to uppercase using the toUpperCase() method. After that, we check if the hex is only one character long. If it is, we add a leading zero using the string concatenation operator (+), so that it's two characters long. Finally, we return the original value parameter concatenated with the alpha hex value.

If you want to write your JavaScript code as compact as possible, you can use the following version:

```
part_1/adding_transparency_to_hex/adding_transparency_to_hex_ex2.js
function addAlphaToHex(hex, percent) {
  const alpha = Math.round(percent / 100 * 255).toString(16)
              .toUpperCase().padStart(2, "0");
  return hex + alpha;
}

addAlphaToHex("#FFFFFF", 70);      // → "#FFFFFFB3"
```

This version combines the rgb and alpha constants into one line and uses pad-Start() to add a leading zero if necessary. The first parameter of padStart() defines the length of the resulting string once the given string has been padded, so padStart(2, "0") ensures the hex string is always two characters long.

If you want to view your colors in different formats, you can use the Chrome/Edge DevTools. Open the DevTools panel and navigate to the styles section to find the color you want to check. Then, click the box located to the left of the color to directly adjust its values:

You can also hold the Shift key and click on the box to switch between different format options, with the values automatically converted.

Removing HTML Tags from Text with DOMParser()

Task

Imagine you've written a web scraper that collects news from the web. The text you grab may contain unwanted HTML elements, like <span>, <img>, <a>, etc.

What's worse, it may contain injected JavaScript code that automatically gets executed once you put it on your website. What you need is a function that safely removes all unwanted elements from the text.

Solution

Use the parseFromString() method from the DOMParser() interface to parse the string. Once you parse the string, you can use the textContent property to get the text free from any extra HTML tags:

```
part_1/removing_html_tags/DOMParser_ex1.js
function stripHTML(html){
  const doc = new DOMParser().parseFromString(html, "text/html");
  return doc.body.textContent || "";
}

const rawText = '<a href="">Fed</a> Signals<img src="n.png"> Smaller Rises';

stripHTML(rawText);     // → "Fed Signals Smaller Rises"
```

The DOMParser interface lets you parse XML or HTML code from a string into a DOM Document. In this case, you want to parse HTML, so you pass text/html as the second argument. The result is an HTMLDocument whose text you can extract with textContent.

DOMParser() in Node

⚠ The DOMParser() interface is not available in the Node environment.

Discussion

The `textContent` property is available on all text and element nodes. So why parse HTML when you can create a temporary element on the page and get its `textContent`? Consider this example:

part_1/removing_html_tags/DOMParser_ex2.js
```js
// Don't use this
function stripHTML(html) {
  const tmp = document.createElement("DIV");
  tmp.innerHTML = html;
  return tmp.textContent || "";
}

const rawText = '<a href="">Fed</a> Signals<img src="n.png"> Smaller Rises';

stripHTML(rawText);     // → "Fed Signals Smaller Rises"
```

At first glance, this code seems like a more efficient solution because it doesn't involve parsing the string. But if the source contains malicious code, you'll leave your code wide open to attacks.

Try to strip the following text from HTML, and you'll see that the JavaScript code hidden in the onerror attribute gets executed:

part_1/removing_html_tags/DOMParser_ex3.js
```js
const rawText = "<img onerror='alert(\"execute JS here\")' src=untrusted>";
```

Although you're inserting the text into a temporary tag, the browser still loads the image, and the embedded JavaScript code gets a chance to rear its head.

Remember to remove HTML tags from the text when scraping and using text from external sources. A quick way to do that is to use the DOMParser interface to parse the data and then extract text with `textContent`.

Recipe 8

Converting HTML Markup to HTML Entities with replaceAll()

Task

Imagine you want to publish programming tutorials on your website that contain HTML markup. But you encounter an issue where web browsers interpret the HTML tags in your examples instead of displaying them. This happens because browsers assume that you use the tags to structure your web page.

You need to represent the markup in a way that prevents the browser from interpreting it.

Solution

Use the replaceAll() method to replace the components of HTML tags with entities:

part_1/converting_html_to_entities/entities_ex1.js
```
function escapeHTML(str) {
  return str
    .replaceAll('&', '&amp;')
    .replaceAll('<', '&lt;')
    .replaceAll('>', '&gt;')
    .replaceAll('"', '&quot;')
    .replaceAll("'", '&apos;');
}
escapeHTML('<a href="test.htm">foo</a>');
// → "&lt;a href=&quot;test.htm&quot;&gt;foo&lt;/a&gt;"
```

replaceAll() lets you replace all occurrences of a pattern in a string. With each call, it returns a new string so you can chain multiple replaceAll() methods to replace several patterns in a single statement.

Discussion

By using HTML entities, we can display certain characters that would otherwise be interpreted by web browsers as HTML code. The table below shows the list of characters and their respective HTML entities:

Character	Entity
&	&amp;
<	&lt;
>	&gt;
"	&quot;
'	&apos;

Keep in mind that HTML entities are case sensitive, so & and & are not the same entity.

There are two types of HTML entities: named entities and numeric entities. Named entities are represented by a string of letters enclosed in an ampersand (&) and a semicolon (;). Numeric entities, on the other hand, are represented by an ampersand (&), followed by a pound sign (#), and either a decimal or hexadecimal code, and end with a semicolon (;).

Here's the table above with the named entities converted to their corresponding numeric entities:

Character	Entity
&	&
<	<
>	>
"	"
'	'

You can use both named and numeric entities to display special characters in HTML documents. But named entities are generally preferred over numeric ones because they are more human-readable and easier to remember.

Besides displaying characters that have special meanings, HTML entities are also useful to display characters that are difficult to type using a standard keyboard, such as foreign language characters, mathematical symbols, or emojis. By using HTML entities, we can ensure that these characters are displayed correctly on web pages.

Recipe 9

Intersecting HTML Tables with filter()

Task

Let's say you have a sports app that displays statistics and scores. You have two objects and want to find properties that exist in both objects simultaneously. Your first object contains a list of national teams that have won the FIFA World Cup along with the total number of wins. Your second object includes similar information about the UEFA European Football Championship.

You want to create an HTML table that lists the intersection of the two objects, that is, a table of teams that have won at least one cup in both competitions.

Solution

The first step is to create an HTML table. You can delegate this task to JavaScript, but let's keep it simple by having an HTML structure in place and using JavaScript to insert information into the table:

```
part_1/intersecting_tables/filter_ex1.html
<table id="national_teams">
  <thead>
    <tr>
      <th>Country</th>
      <th>UEFA Wins</th>
      <th>FIFA Wins</th>
    </tr>
  </thead>
  <tbody></tbody>
</table>
```

Now create two objects: one for FIFA champions and one for UEFA champions, like this:

```
part_1/intersecting_tables/filter_ex1.js
const FIFAChamps = {
  "Brazil": 5,
  "Germany": 4,
  "Italy": 4,
  "Argentina": 2,
  "France": 2,
  "Uruguay": 2,
  "Spain": 1,
  "England": 1
};

const UEFAChamps = {
  "Germany": 3,
  "Spain": 3,
  "Italy": 2,
  "France": 2,
  "Russia": 1,
  "Czech Republic": 1,
  "Portugal": 1,
  "Netherlands": 1,
  "Denmark": 1,
  "Greece": 1
};
```

To perform an intersection, obtain the keys of the first object with Object.keys()[7] and then check which keys are present in the second object with filter():[8]

part_1/intersecting_tables/filter_ex1.js

```javascript
function getIntersection(obj1, obj2) {
  return Object.keys(obj1).filter(key => {
    return key in obj2;
  });
}

// This constant will hold an array containing the keys of intersection
const intersection = getIntersection(FIFAChamps, UEFAChamps);

// Get a reference to the body of the table
const tbody = document.querySelector("#national_teams tbody");

intersection.forEach(elem => {
  const row = tbody.insertRow();
  const cell1 = row.insertCell(0);
  const cell2 = row.insertCell(1);
  const cell3 = row.insertCell(2);
  cell1.textContent = elem;
  cell2.textContent = UEFAChamps[elem];
  cell3.textContent = FIFAChamps[elem];
});
```

Once you get the intersection of the two objects, loop over the properties, and each time through the loop, insert the team, UEFA wins, and FIFA wins into the first, second, and third cell, respectively. Here, we're using JavaScript's built-in methods, including insertRow() and insertCell(), to create table rows and cells, but you can use string literals too. Here's the result after applying some basic CSS styling:

Country	UEFA Wins	FIFA Wins
Germany	3	4
Italy	2	4
France	2	2
Spain	3	1

The table lists only countries that exist in both objects simultaneously.

---

7. https://developer.mozilla.org/en-US/docs/Web/JavaScript/Reference/Global_Objects/Object/keys
8. https://developer.mozilla.org/en-US/docs/Web/JavaScript/Reference/Global_Objects/Array/filter

Discussion

The filter() method takes a function as an argument and executes it for each element of an array—similar to forEach() and map(). The function you supply should be a predicate (a function that returns true or false). filter() will add an element to the resulting array only if the return value of your predicate is true.

When using the filter() method in JavaScript, it's important to remember that it skips over any missing elements in arrays. For example, if you have an array with gaps such as [0, 1, , , 4, , 6], you can take advantage of filter() to get rid of the missing elements like this:

```
const sparseArr = [0, 1, , , 4, , 6];
sparseArr.filter(() => true);    // → [ 0, 1, 4, 6 ]
```

Here we use an arrow function that always returns true. Since filter() skips gaps, the new array won't be sparse.

If your array also has undefined and null elements, you can remove them with filter() too:

```
const sparseArr = [0, 1, , null, 4, undefined, 6];
sparseArr.filter(x => x !== undefined && x !== null);    // → [ 0, 1, 4, 6 ]
```

In this code, we use the strict inequality operator (!==) to return true only if the element isn't null or undefined.

When it comes to performance optimization, you should take into account the size of your objects and the number of times you'd need to get their intersection. If your first object has 1000 properties and your second object has 50, your code will run faster if you get the keys of the object with fewer properties and then apply a filter, not the other way around.

With this in mind, let's rewrite our intersection function:

```
part_1/intersecting_tables/filter_ex2.js
Line 1  function getIntersection(obj1, obj2) {
     2    const k1 = Object.keys(obj1);
     3    const k2 = Object.keys(obj2);
     4    const [first, next] = k1.length > k2.length ? [k2, obj1] : [k1, obj2];
     5    return first.filter(key => key in next);
     6  }
```

Notice how we used a ternary operator on the right hand of the destructuring assignment to compare the length of objects and assign the one with fewer properties to first (line 4). Destructuring enables us to extract values and assign them to variables using a syntax that is similar to array literals. On the right side of the assignment is the data to be destructured. On the left side is the variables that will receive the data.

Our function now works faster when dealing with large arrays. But, remember, such micro-optimization is helpful only for performance-critical applications. In most cases, you'd be okay with the original solution in this recipe.

Recipe 10

Generating HTML Tables from an Array of Arrays

Task

Suppose your task is to generate reports or summaries of data that are stored in an array of arrays. For instance, you may need to create a summary of performance metrics for a company across multiple financial quarters from an array like this:

```
const data = [
  ["Quarter", "Revenue", "Eps"],
  ["Q1 FY22", 45962, 2.71],
  ["Q2 FY22", 44845, 2.71],
  ["Q3 FY22", 46151, 2.03],
  ["Q4 FY22", 46822, 2.11],
  ["Q1 FY23", 45215, 2.64]
];
```

Your objective is to convert the array into an HTML table so that you can present the data in a structured and organized format.

Solution

Use the following function:

part_1/generating_html_table_v1/html_table_v1_ex1.js
```
const data = [
  ["Quarter", "Revenue", "Eps"],
  ["Q1 FY22", 45962, 2.71],
  ["Q2 FY22", 44845, 2.71],
  ["Q3 FY22", 46151, 2.03],
  ["Q4 FY22", 46822, 2.11],
  ["Q1 FY23", 45215, 2.64]
];
```

```
function createTable(data) {
  const table = document.createElement("table");
  const thead = table.createTHead();
  const tbody = table.createTBody();
  const headerRow = thead.insertRow();

  // Create table head
  data[0].forEach(item => {
    const th = document.createElement("th");
    th.innerText = item;
    headerRow.appendChild(th);
  });

  // Create table body
  data.slice(1).forEach(rowData => {
    const row = tbody.insertRow();
    rowData.forEach(item => {
      const cell = row.insertCell();
      cell.innerText = item;
    });
  });

  document.body.appendChild(table);
}

createTable(data);
```

The createTable() function takes an array of arrays as its argument and creates an HTML table with the data. Here's the output after applying some basic styling:

Quarter	Revenue	Eps
Q1 FY22	45962	2.71
Q2 FY22	44845	2.71
Q3 FY22	46151	2.03
Q4 FY22	46822	2.11
Q1 FY23	45215	2.64

Discussion

We begin by creating an HTML table element using the createElement() method. We then create three more elements: a thead element (to hold the table header row), a tbody element (to hold the table body rows), and a row element (to hold the thead data).

In this recipe, we assume that the column headers for the table are contained in the first sub-array of the data array. So, we loop through each item in the first sub-array, create a new th element using the createElement() method, set the innerText property of the th element to the current item, and append the th element to the previously created header row.

After creating the header row, we then loop through each sub-array of the data array except the first one (in other words, all the rows of data except the header row). We use the slice() method to set aside the first sub-array. For each row, we create a new tr element within the tbody element and loop through each item in the rowData, creating a new td element for each item, and setting its innerText property to the current item.

Finally, we append the entire table element (including the header and body rows) to the body of the HTML document using the appendChild() method. Make sure to modify this line to append the data to the element you want.

If you have data in an array that you want to display in a tabular format on a web page, converting it to an HTML table can make it easier for users to read and understand.

Recipe 11

Generating HTML Tables from an Array of Objects

Task

Suppose your task is to generate reports of data that are stored in an array of objects like the following:

```
const data = [
  {quarter: "Q1 FY22", revenue: 45962, netIncome: 20820, eps: 2.71},
  {quarter: "Q2 FY22", revenue: 44845, netIncome: 20610, eps: 2.71},
  {quarter: "Q3 FY22", revenue: 46151, netIncome: 16027, eps: 2.03},
  {quarter: "Q4 FY22", revenue: 46822, netIncome: 16244, eps: 2.11},
  {quarter: "Q1 FY23", revenue: 45215, netIncome: 20256, eps: 2.64}
];
```

In the previous recipe, you created a table using an array of arrays. But, for this recipe, the data is stored in an array of objects. This means that you need to use a slightly different approach to generate a table.

Solution

Use the following function:

part_1/generating_html_table_v2/html_table_v2_ex1.js

```js
const data = [
  {quarter: "Q1 FY22", revenue: 45962, netIncome: 20820, eps: 2.71},
  {quarter: "Q2 FY22", revenue: 44845, netIncome: 20610, eps: 2.71},
  {quarter: "Q3 FY22", revenue: 46151, netIncome: 16027, eps: 2.03},
  {quarter: "Q4 FY22", revenue: 46822, netIncome: 16244, eps: 2.11},
  {quarter: "Q1 FY23", revenue: 45215, netIncome: 20256, eps: 2.64}
];

const headers = [
  "Quarter",
  "Revenue (in millions of US dollars)",
  "Net Income (in millions of US dollars)",
  "Earnings per Share (EPS)"
];

function createTable(data, headers) {
  const table = document.createElement("table");
  const thead = table.createTHead();
  const tbody = table.createTBody();
  const headerRow = thead.insertRow();

  // Create table head
  headers.forEach(header => {
    const th = document.createElement("th");
    th.innerText = header;
    headerRow.appendChild(th);
  });

  // Create table body
  data.forEach(data => {
    const row = tbody.insertRow();
    Object.values(data).forEach(value => {
      const cell = row.insertCell();
      cell.innerText = value;
    });
  });

  document.body.appendChild(table);
}

createTable(data, headers);
```

When we call this function with the data array as the argument, it generates an HTML table displaying the company's financial performance data. The output will look like the table on page 28 after applying some basic styling.

Quarter	Revenue (in millions of US dollars)	Net Income (in millions of US dollars)	Earnings per Share (EPS)
Q1 FY22	45962	20820	2.71
Q2 FY22	44845	20610	2.71
Q3 FY22	46151	16027	2.03
Q4 FY22	46822	16244	2.11
Q1 FY23	45215	20256	2.64

Discussion

This recipe is similar to the previous one except that the array items are objects, with each object having properties such as revenue, netIncome, and eps. In this recipe, we also define a separate array containing the column headers for the table that we'll be creating.

First, we create a table header (thead) and a table body (tbody) for the table. We then create a header row (headerRow) within the header and populate it with the headers from the headers array.

For each header in the array, we create a th element using the createElement() method, set its content to the header string using the innerText property, and append it to the header row using the appendChild() method.

After creating the header row, we loop through each object in the data array and create a new row in the table body for each object. Within each row, we loop through each property of the object and create a new cell in the row for each property value.

Finally, we append the table element to the HTML body element. You should modify this line to append the data to the element you want.

Recipe 12

Displaying Tabular Data in Console with console.table()

Task

Suppose you have been performing additions and subtractions on an array, but you are encountering some problems. You want to inspect the contents of the array at a particular line in your script so you can pinpoint the problem.

You need a way to quickly print the array's content to the console.

Solution

Use the console.table() method:

```
part_1/displaying_tabular_data/displaying_tabular_data_ex1.js
const data = [
  {quarter: "Q1 FY22", revenue: 45962, netIncome: 20820, eps: 2.71},
  {quarter: "Q2 FY22", revenue: 44845, netIncome: 20610, eps: 2.71},
  {quarter: "Q3 FY22", revenue: 46151, netIncome: 16027, eps: 2.03},
  {quarter: "Q4 FY22", revenue: 46822, netIncome: 16244, eps: 2.11},
  {quarter: "Q1 FY23", revenue: 45215, netIncome: 20256, eps: 2.64}
];

console.table(data);
```

The console.table() method outputs an array in a readable format for human interpretation on the console:

(index)	quarter	revenue	netIncome	eps
0	'Q1 FY22'	45962	20820	2.71
1	'Q2 FY22'	44845	20610	2.71
2	'Q3 FY22'	46151	16027	2.03
3	'Q4 FY22'	46822	16244	2.11
4	'Q1 FY23'	45215	20256	2.64

Discussion

The console.table() method deserves more recognition from JavaScript developers. While many developers use a for loop to log an array's items to the console, JavaScript already has the console.table() method that provides a more straightforward approach to achieve the same result.

The table's initial column will be designated as (index). If the data is in the form of an array, its values will correspond to the array indices. On the other hand, if the data is in the form of an object, its values will align with the property names as shown in the table on page 30.

```
part_1/displaying_tabular_data/displaying_tabular_data_ex2.js
const data = {
  "Q1 FY22": {revenue: 45962, netIncome: 20820, eps: 2.71},
  "Q2 FY22": {revenue: 44845, netIncome: 20610, eps: 2.71},
  "Q3 FY22": {revenue: 46151, netIncome: 16027, eps: 2.03},
  "Q4 FY22": {revenue: 46822, netIncome: 16244, eps: 2.11},
  "Q1 FY23": {revenue: 45215, netIncome: 20256, eps: 2.64}
};

console.table(data);
```

(index)	revenue	netIncome	eps
Q1 FY22	45962	20820	2.71
Q2 FY22	44845	20610	2.71
Q3 FY22	46151	16027	2.03
Q4 FY22	46822	16244	2.11
Q1 FY23	45215	20256	2.64

Here, the quarter value is used as the table heading, and the object with revenue, netIncome, and eps properties is used as the row value.

The console.table() method also takes one additional optional parameter that lets you restrict the columns displayed. For example, if you want to only display the the netIncome column, you can use this:

part_1/displaying_tabular_data/displaying_tabular_data_ex3.js

```
const data = {
  "Q1 FY22": {revenue: 45962, netIncome: 20820, eps: 2.71},
  "Q2 FY22": {revenue: 44845, netIncome: 20610, eps: 2.71},
  "Q3 FY22": {revenue: 46151, netIncome: 16027, eps: 2.03},
  "Q4 FY22": {revenue: 46822, netIncome: 16244, eps: 2.11},
  "Q1 FY23": {revenue: 45215, netIncome: 20256, eps: 2.64}
};

console.table(data, "netIncome");
```

(index)	netIncome
Q1 FY22	20820
Q2 FY22	20610
Q3 FY22	16027
Q4 FY22	16244
Q1 FY23	20256

The console.table() method enables you to generate a clear and concise plaintext representation of tabular data. The benefit of using console.table() becomes particularly apparent when dealing with multidimensional arrays (that is, arrays that comprise other arrays). Remember to take advantage of it when debugging arrays and objects.

Recipe 13

Formatting Dates with Intl.DateTimeFormat()

Task

Suppose you work as a programmer for an online shop that delivers products after two days from the date of purchase. Your task is to create a JavaScript code that will notify the user about the exact day of the week when they can expect to receive their ordered goods.

For instance, if a customer purchases a product on a Saturday, your code should inform them that the delivery will take place on the following Monday.

Solution

This task involves three steps:

- Getting the current date
- Adding two days to the current date
- Converting that date to the day of the week

We can perform the first two steps with a function like this:

```
function addDaysToToday(days) {
  const d = new Date();
  d.setDate(d.getDate() + days);
  return d;
}

const dayAfterTomorrow = addDaysToToday(2);

console.log(dayAfterTomorrow);
// → Wed Apr 12 2023 11:41:09 GMT+0400
```

First, use the Date() constructor to get the current date. Next, retrieve the day of the month for today by calling the getDate() method of the date object. Add two to this value to get the day after tomorrow's date. Then, use the setDate() method to update the day of the month, and the date object will automatically adjust the month and year if needed.

After performing the preceding steps, you'll have a string that contains the date after tomorrow, along with the timestamp and timezone. But you need only the day and the month and don't want to include the timestamp or timezone. So, use the Intl.DateTimeFormat() constructor to format the date:

```javascript
function getFormattedDate(locale, date) {
  const formatter = new Intl.DateTimeFormat(locale, {dateStyle: "full"});
  return formatter.format(date);
}

const formattedDate = getFormattedDate("en-US", dayAfterTomorrow)

console.log(formattedDate);
// → Wednesday, April 12, 2023
```

Intl.DateTimeFormat() accepts an object as its second argument that specifies how the date should be formatted. In this case, you want to include the day of the week in the date, so set the dateStyle to full.

Here's how the final code should look like:

part_1/formatting_dates/adding_days_ex1.js
```javascript
function addDaysToToday(days) {
  const d = new Date();
  d.setDate(d.getDate() + days);
  return d;
}

function getFormattedDate(locale, date) {
  const formatter = new Intl.DateTimeFormat(locale, {dateStyle: "full"});
  return formatter.format(date);
}

const dayAfterTomorrow = addDaysToToday(2);
const msg = "We'll deliver your purchase on ";

console.log(msg + getFormattedDate("en-US", dayAfterTomorrow));
// → We'll deliver your purchase on Wednesday, April 12, 2023
```

This code generates a message containing the expected delivery date of a purchase based on the current date and a specified locale.

Discussion

To ensure that the date format in your application is suitable for the country where the products are being shipped, you should pass an appropriate BCP 47 language tag to Intl.DateTimeFormat().[9]

---

9.   https://www.iana.org/assignments/language-subtag-registry/language-subtag-registry

A language tag is composed of one or more subtags, which identify the language, script, region, and other language-related information. For example, "en-GB" is a language tag that represents British English, where "en" indicates the language and "GB" indicates the region. The BCP-47 standard is widely used in software development to ensure consistent language support across different platforms.

In this solution, we've used the "en-US" language to indicate American English. But, if you're delivering a product to France, for example, you should use the "fr-FR" tag to indicate the French language:

```
part_1/formatting_dates/adding_days_ex2.js
function addDaysToToday(days) {
  const d = new Date();
  d.setDate(d.getDate() + days);
  return d;
}

function getFormattedDate(locale, date) {
  const formatter = new Intl.DateTimeFormat(locale, {dateStyle: "full"});
  return formatter.format(date);
}

const dayAfterTomorrow = addDaysToToday(2);
const msg = "Nous livrerons votre achat ";

console.log(msg + getFormattedDate("fr-FR", dayAfterTomorrow));
// → Nous livrerons votre achat mercredi 12 avril 2023
```

Converting a String to a Date Object

If you want to scrape a date from text and turn it into a Date object, you can use the Date() constructor.[10]

Consider using the Intl.DateTimeFormat() constructor when working with date and time. Intl.DateTimeFormat() lets you get date formatting for different languages, set the style for date and time, define a numbering system for languages such as Thai and Arabic, and more. For a complete list of available options, visit MDN Web Docs.[11]

---

10. https://developer.mozilla.org/en-US/docs/Web/JavaScript/Reference/Global_Objects/Date/Date
11. https://developer.mozilla.org/en-US/docs/Web/JavaScript/Reference/Global_Objects/Intl/DateTimeFormat/Date-TimeFormat

Recipe 14

Formatting Currencies with Intl.NumberFormat()

Task

Imagine you run an online shop that delivers products to various countries. You want to display the prices of the items in the currency of the user's location. So, for example, if a visitor from Canada chooses to view a monitor priced at $499 in U.S. dollars, you want to automatically 1) convert the price from USD to CAD and 2) format the currency according to CAD.

Solution

First, you need to obtain the exchange rate between the U.S. dollar (USD) and the Canadian dollar (CAD). Since the rate can vary constantly, you should use an online API that gives you real-time data for the currencies you want to convert. These services usually require a paid subscription.

In this recipe, we'll use the free service available at exchangerate.host, which updates the exchange rates only once a day. You can send a fetch request to the API by specifying the currencies you want to convert as parameters.

Once the fetch is successful, read and parse the data using the json() method, like this:

```
async function getExchangeRate(from, to) {
  const api = `https://api.exchangerate.host/convert?from=${from}&to=${to}`;
  let response = await fetch(api);
  response = await response.json();
  return response.info.rate;
}

const exchangeRate = getExchangeRate("USD", "CAD");
```

Now that you have an exchange rate for your target currency, you need a way to format it. Pass the ISO code of the currency you want to convert to the Intl.NumberFormat() constructor as an option. This will return an object that has a format() method which you can use to format any amount:

```
function getFormattedCurrency(currency, amount) {
  return new Intl.NumberFormat("en-US", {
    style: "currency",
    currency: currency,
```

```
  }).format(amount);
}

getFormattedCurrency("CAD", exchangeRate * 499)
```

After some cleanup, your final code should look like this:

part_1/formatting_currencies/NumberFormat_ex1.js
```
const USDprice = 499;

async function getExchangeRate(from, to) {
  const api = `https://api.exchangerate.host/convert?from=${from}&to=${to}`;
  let response = await fetch(api);
  response = await response.json();
  return response.info.rate;
}
function getFormattedCurrency(currency, amount) {
  return new Intl.NumberFormat("en-CA", {
    style: "currency",
    currency: currency,
  }).format(amount);
}

getExchangeRate("USD", "CAD").then(exchangeRate => {
  console.log(getFormattedCurrency("CAD", exchangeRate * USDprice));
});

// Logs something like:
// → CA$679.31
```

TypeError

 If you're getting an error like "TypeError: Failed to fetch," it's likely because you're running the code in your browser's console. Unless you're on https://exchangerate.host/, your browser's security mechanism will block the request. Try executing the code in an HTML document or the Node environment (requires Node v18).

Discussion

As with every other method in the Internationalization API, Intl.NumberFormat() takes a BCP 47 language tag as its first argument.[12] Here, the language tag tells the method what locale to use when formatting currencies, which is useful when you want to offer your website in multiple languages.

For example, if you pass "ar" as a language tag, the resulting number will be in the Arabic alphabet:

---

12. https://www.iana.org/assignments/language-subtag-registry/language-subtag-registry

part_1/formatting_currencies/NumberFormat_ex2.js

```
function getFormattedCurrency(currency, amount) {
  return new Intl.NumberFormat("ar", {
    style: "currency",
    currency: currency,
  }).format(amount);
}

getFormattedCurrency("SAR", 499);      // → "٤٩٩٫٠٠ ر.س"
```

You can further refine how the currency is displayed by setting options in the second argument. A useful option is signDisplay which lets you set when to display the sign for the number.

By default, the function displays a sign for negative numbers only (including negative zero, which is a negative number that has been rounded to zero). If you want to always display the sign, such as when indicating a change in balance, you should use "always":

part_1/formatting_currencies/NumberFormat_ex3.js

```
function getFormattedCurrency(currency, amount) {
  return new Intl.NumberFormat("en", {
    style: "currency",
    currency: currency,
    signDisplay: "always"
  }).format(amount);
}

getFormattedCurrency("USD", 499);      // → "+$499.00"
```

The Intl.NumberFormat() constructor makes it easy to deal with numbers in JavaScript. Remember to take advantage of it whenever you need to format currencies.

Recipe 15

Adding Thousand Separators to Numbers with Intl.NumberFormat()

Task

Suppose you aim to add a thousands separator to numbers consisting of four or more digits. Perhaps you are retrieving financial data from a database to use in an article for a finance publication that is published in multiple languages.

Thousand separators are used in many different languages and countries to make large numbers easier to read. However, the character used as the thousand separator can vary across languages and cultures.

For example, let's say you have the following string:

1000000000

And you'd like to format it as:

1,000,000,000

You need to write code to add thousand separators programmatically to the number.

Solution

Use the Intl.NumberFormat() constructor:

```
part_1/adding_thousand_separators/adding_thousand_separators_ex1.js
function addThousandSeparator(num, locale) {
  const numFormat = new Intl.NumberFormat(locale);
  return numFormat.format(num);
}

addThousandSeparator(1000000000, "en");
// → "1,000,000,000"
```

In this code, new Intl.NumberFormat() creates a NumberFormat object. Then, the format() method is called on the object, passing the "en" argument to specify the English language. The function returns a formatted string with thousand separators added based on the locale.

Discussion

Including thousand separators in numerical values is an easy way to enhance the clarity and visual appeal of your data. But, it's crucial to verify the type of the content before proceeding.

The comma (,) is commonly used as a thousand separator in English-speaking countries and many other countries. For example, 10,000,000 represents ten million. However, in many European countries, such as Germany, Greece, and Italy, the period (.) is used as the thousand separator and the comma (,) is used as the decimal separator. So, to represent ten million, they use 10.000.000.

In some countries, other symbols or characters are used as the thousand separator. For example, the Indian numbering system uses a comma-like symbol called a "separator" to separate groups of digits. While the Chinese and Japanese numeral systems use different characters to represent thousands, millions, and other large numbers.

Generally, numbers that are less than 1000 don't need separators. Also, numbers in scientific notation, postal codes, and phones do not require separators for clarity. As a result, documents and data that consist of such numbers may not be suitable for automatic comma inclusion.

The solution in this recipe can be adapted to add thousand separators to numbers in various numeral systems. For instance, to include thousand separators following the German language conventions, you can pass "de-DE" (a BCP-47 language tag) to the NumberFormat() constructor, as shown below:

```
part_1/adding_thousand_separators/adding_thousand_separators_ex2.js
function addThousandSeparator(num, locale) {
  const numFormat = new Intl.NumberFormat(locale);
  return numFormat.format(num);
}

addThousandSeparator(1000000000, "de-DE");
// → "1.000.000.000"
```

Remember, the thousand separator character is not universal and may differ across countries and written languages. Also, the specific formatting conventions may vary depending on the context, such as in scientific notation, where commas are generally not used. To extract a number with thousand separators from a string, see Recipe 69, Matching Formatted Numbers with Thousand Separators, on page 175.

Recipe 16

Creating Language-Sensitive Lists with Intl.ListFormat()

Task

Let's say you have a gaming app and want to display the top three players of the week based on their scores. Because your app is available in multiple languages, you need a function that can format the list automatically based on the user's language preference. It's fairly common to have a series of items like this stored in an array that you need to format as a sentence in different languages.

Solution

Use the Intl.ListFormat() constructor:

part_1/creating_lists/ListFormat_ex1.js

```
const topPlayers = ["Kraken", "Boss99", "Ninja"];
const msg = "Congratulations to this week's winners: ";

function getFormattedList(lang, arr) {
  const formatter = new Intl.ListFormat(lang, {type: "conjunction"});
  return formatter.format(arr);
}

console.log(msg + getFormattedList("en", topPlayers));

// logs:
// → Congratulations to this week's winners: Kraken, Boss99, and Ninja
```

This function returns a formatted string representation of the array items based on the specified language.

Browser Compatibility

Support for ListFormat was added in Safari 14.1 on macOS and Safari 14.5 on iOS.[13] So, although all modern browsers support ListFormat, users who haven't updated their browsers for a while won't be able to run your app. For maximum compatibility, use this API with a polyfill,[14] or on the server side (available since Node version 13.0.0).

Discussion

The ECMAScript Internationalization API enables us to develop applications that can adapt to different languages. To access this API, we use the Intl namespace. In the example, we used the Intl.ListFormat() constructor of the API, which provides a straightforward way to format lists in a way that is culturally appropriate.

We begin by creating a function called getFormattedList() that takes two arguments: lang and arr. lang is a BCP 47 language tag that represents the language

---

13. https://caniuse.com/mdn-javascript_builtins_intl_listformat_format
14. https://github.com/wessberg/intl-list-format

code of the locale to be used for formatting the list, and arr is an array of items to be formatted.[15]

Inside the function, we create an instance of Intl.ListFormat, which takes two arguments: lang and an options object. In this case, we want to format the list for the English language, so we pass "en" as the language tag. The options object specifies the type of conjunction to be used to join the items in the list. We specify that the conjunction "and" should be used to join the items in the list by setting {type: "conjunction"}.

Finally, we call the formatter.format(arr) method on the Intl.ListFormat object with the arr argument passed in. This method returns a formatted string representation of the array items based on the specified language and conjunction type that we set earlier.

To format the list in a different language, we can simply pass the relevant language tag to the function. For instance, if we want to format the list in Spanish, we can call the function with the argument "es."

Here is an example output of the function when the language argument is set to "es":

```
part_1/creating_lists/ListFormat_ex2.js
const topPlayers = ["Kraken", "Boss99", "Ninja"];
const msg = "Felicidades a los ganadores de esta semana: ";

function getFormattedList(lang, arr) {
  const formatter = new Intl.ListFormat(lang, {type: "conjunction"});
  return formatter.format(arr);
}

console.log(msg + getFormattedList("es", topPlayers));

// logs:
// → Felicidades a los ganadores de esta semana: Kraken, Boss99 y Ninja
```

The Intl.ListFormat() constructor comes in handy even if we want to format lists only in English because it eliminates possible grammatical errors. For example, if we have only two items in an array, it won't add a comma before "and":

```
part_1/creating_lists/ListFormat_ex3.js
const topPlayers = ["Kraken", "Boss99"];
const msg = "Congratulations to this week's winners: ";
```

---

15. https://www.iana.org/assignments/language-subtag-registry/language-subtag-registry

```
function getFormattedList(lang, arr) {
  const formatter = new Intl.ListFormat(lang, {type: "conjunction"});
  return formatter.format(arr);
}
console.log(msg + getFormattedList("en", topPlayers));

// logs:
// → Congratulations to this week's winners: Kraken and Boss99
```

The second argument of the ListFormat method is optional and lets us set options such as the style and type of grouping. The default value of type is a conjunction, but if we want to do an "or"-based grouping of the list items, we can use disjunction.

For example, perhaps we want to ask players which honorary title they prefer: Legendary, Mighty, or Bold. So then the app will append that title to their name like "Faraz the Mighty":

part_1/creating_lists/ListFormat_ex4.js
```
const titles = ["Legendary", "Mighty", "Bold"];
const formatter = new Intl.ListFormat("en", {type: "disjunction"});

console.log("Which honorary title do you prefer? " +
            formatter.format(titles));

// logs:
// → Which honorary title do you prefer? Legendary, Mighty, or Bold
```

There's also an option that lets us group the list items as a unit:

part_1/creating_lists/ListFormat_ex5.js
```
const titles = ["Legendary", "Mighty", "Bold"];
const formatter = new Intl.ListFormat("en", {type: "unit"});

console.log(formatter.format(titles));

// logs:
// → Legendary, Mighty, Bold
```

This example sets the value of type as unit, so it formats the list with no "and" or "or."

Whenever you want to list a series of items in a sentence, consider using the ListFormat constructor, as it properly takes care of punctuation in English or other languages.

Recipe 17

Determining Letter Case with charAt()

Task

Consider a scenario where you have a form that requests the user to enter their nickname. Some users may prefer to enter their nickname in lowercase letters, so your app shouldn't automatically capitalize the nickname. But perhaps some users are casual about typing and intend for their name to be capitalized.

In such cases, you want to notify the user that their nickname will be stored and displayed exactly as entered. So, your app needs to be capable of identifying the letter case of the first character of the nickname.

Solution

Use the strict inequality operator (!==) to compare the first character (index 0) of the string to its lowercase version. If they are not equal, that means the string starts with a capital letter:

```
part_1/determining_letter_case/charAt_ex1.js
function isCapital(str) {
  return str.charAt(0) !== str.charAt(0).toLowerCase();
}

isCapital("Dave");    // → true
isCapital("dave");    // → false
```

Success! You are now able to determine the letter case of the first character of a word.

Discussion

The function in this recipe returns true if the first character of the input string is in uppercase and false otherwise. To get the first letter of the input string, we use the charAt() method. This method takes an index number as an argument and returns the character at the given position in a string. For instance, "Hello".charAt(1) returns the second character of "Hello" which is "e."

You may be wondering why not use the strict equality operator (===) to compare the character with its uppercase version.

To understand why, let's rewrite the example with ===:

```
// Don't use this code

function isCapital(str) {
  return str.charAt(0) === str.charAt(0).toUpperCase();
}
isCapital("dave");          // → false
isCapital("1990Dave");      // → true

// Arabic name
isCapital("أمير");          // → true

// Hebrew name
isCapital("אליהו");         // → true
```

This version of the function will return true even if the input string starts with a number, such as "1990Dave". toUpperCase() has no effect on the characters in the input string that do not have an uppercase version. So, in this example, we're comparing the equality of "1" with the same string "1" after converting it to uppercase. As a result, the comparison returns true.

The function will also return true for languages like Hebrew and Arabic, which don't have uppercase and lowercase letters.

There's a caveat when using charAt() with specific languages that have *supplementary characters*, such as Chinese. To be able to represent these characters, JavaScript has to allocate more "spaces" in a string, which causes charAt() to fail:

```
// Notice how the return value of charAt() isn't
// recognizable at index 0 and index 1

const str = "𠮷";

console.log(str.length);      // → 2
console.log(str.charAt(0));   // → ♦
console.log(str.charAt(1));   // → ♦
console.log(str.charAt(2));   // → (empty string)
```

JavaScript uses UTF-16 code points to represent characters, and most characters require one code point. For example, the character "F" is assigned a code point of U+0046.

However, sometimes a character is made of more than one code point. In this case, the Chinese character consists of two Unicode code points. The first one has a value of U+d846, while the second one has a value of U+df10. You can confirm that by preceding each code with a \u and putting both pairs in a string like this:

```
console.log("\ud846\udf10");      // → 𪌐
```

Neither pair corresponds to a printable character on its own, so the charAt() method cannot return a valid character at index 0 or index 1. The fourth console.log() method attempts to get the character at index 2, but since there's no character at that position, it returns an empty string.

Use the charAt() method whenever you need to get a character at a specific index, but be wary of languages with supplementary characters as they can break your code. Fortunately, JavaScript has another method to help you handle supplementary characters, which you'll learn about in the next recipe. To learn more about Unicode, see Appendix 1, What Is Unicode?, on page 191.

Recipe 18

Counting Unicode Characters with Intl.Segmenter()

Task

Let's say you have an app that requires user registration and includes a text input for the user's bio. The bio may be in any language and include emojis. You want to limit the length of the bio to precisely 120 characters. So, you need to calculate the length of the string. Easy! Use the length() method to get the number of characters:

```
console.log("叶".length);      // → 2
console.log("🐈🐈".length);   // → 4
```

This is probably not the result you expected. Strings in JavaScript are based on UTF-16, which represents characters using one or two 16-bit integers. Some characters, such as the Chinese character for kǒu cái (eloquence) and the cat emoji, require two 16-bit units (surrogate pairs) to encode. The length() method gives you the number of UTF-16 code units in a string, not the number of characters.

Supplementary Characters

Characters that are made of a pair of 16-bit surrogate code units are known as supplementary characters.

Solution

Use the Intl.Segmenter() constructor:

```
part_1/counting_characters/char_segmenter_ex2.js
function getLength(str) {
  return [...new Intl.Segmenter().segment(str)].length;
}

getLength("叻");        // → 1
getLength("爤爤");      // → 2
```

This function returns the number of Unicode segments in the input string. In other words, it determines the length of the given string based on the number of Unicode characters, rather than the number of code units.

Browser Compatibility

Segmenter() is a part of the Internationalization API. While most browsers have supported the Internationalization API features for years, Segmenter() is a relatively newer feature that remains unsupported in Firefox (at the time of this writing).[16]

There are some Unicode-aware libraries like Graphemer that let you split JavaScript strings into separate letters,[17] but their results aren't perfectly consistent with those from Segmenter. There's no perfect way to emulate the behavior of Segmenter() in browsers, because doing so requires lots of language-specific rules.

Until browser support is more solid, you can run Intl.Segmenter() on the server side (supported since Node 16).

Discussion

The Intl.Segmenter() constructor allows us to segment a string according to a specified locale and granularity. In this case, we are using the default implementation, so we call the method with no arguments. Because Intl.Segmenter() is a constructor, we need to call it with the new keyword.

The returned object has a segment() method, which accepts a single-string argument. The method segments the string, as its name suggests, meaning that it splits the string into user-perceived character boundaries. Because the returned value is an iterator, we can use the spread syntax (...) to expand

---

16. https://caniuse.com/mdn-javascript_builtins_intl_segmenter_segment
17. https://github.com/flmnt/graphemer

the object into its elements. The spread syntax consists of three dots in a row, and lets us quickly create an array from the iterator.

Finally, we calculate the length of the array to get the number of Unicode characters in the string. If you find the code to be too cryptic, you can use this version instead:

```
part_1/counting_characters/char_segmenter_ex3.js
function getLength(str) {
  // Create a an instance of segmenter
  const Segmenter = new Intl.Segmenter();

  // Segment the string
  const segment = Segmenter.segment(str);

  // Convert it into an array
  const arr = Array.from(segment);

  // Return the number of characters
  return arr.length;
}

getLength("叶");       // → 1
getLength("🐪🐪");     // → 2
```

This version of the code does the exact same operations as the first. You'll probably come across code that uses other techniques to count the number of characters in a string. One technique is to convert the string into an array of characters and then count the number of elements in the array:

```
const str1 = "叶";
const str2 = "🐪🐪";
const str3 = "叶🐪abc";

console.log(Array.from(str1).length);   // → 1
console.log(Array.from(str2).length);   // → 2
console.log(Array.from(str3).length);   // → 5

console.log([...str1].length);          // → 1
console.log([...str2].length);          // → 2
console.log([...str2].length);          // → 5
```

This trick works because strings since ES2015 have built-in iterators that are Unicode-aware and automatically treat a supplementary character as a single value. However, counting the number of characters in a string is not always as simple. In some cases, this technique could give you an inaccurate result. For example:

```
const str = "👨‍👩‍👧";
console.log(Array.from(str).length);    // → 5
console.log([...str].length);           // → 5
```

The family emoji above is known as an Emoji ZWJ Sequence that's made of three independent emojis:

👨‍👩‍👧 = 👨 + 👩 + 👧

These emojis are shown in their connected forms when a zero-width joiner (ZWJ) is placed between them. ZWJ is a non-printing character that causes characters or emojis to be shown in their connected forms on supported platforms.

In the example above, the length of the emoji is 5 because we're counting every ZWJ too. The following code snippet should make this clearer:

```
console.log([..."👨‍👩‍👧"]);  // => ['👨', '', '👩', '', '👧']
```

The empty strings in the result represent ZWJ characters. Since ZWJs are non-printable, they are displayed as empty strings.

Another issue is that some characters look the same but have different code points, and thus are not equal. Consider the following code:

```
const str1 = "é";
const str2 = "é";

console.log(str1 === str2);    // → false

console.log(Array.from(str1).length);    // → 1
console.log(Array.from(str2).length);    // → 2
```

The character assigned to str1 may look exactly the same as the character assigned to str2, but in reality, they're different characters. The character in the first string has a code point of U+00E9 (LATIN SMALL LETTER E WITH ACUTE), while the second character consists of two separate code points, including U+0065 (LATIN SMALL LETTER E) and U+0301 (COMBINING ACUTE ACCENT):

```
console.log("\u00E9");          // → é
console.log("\u0065\u0301");    // → é
```

This explains why the length of the second string is two. Fortunately, the Internationalization API is smart enough to count such characters as a single character. Compare:

```
const str1 = "é";
const str2 = "é";
const str3 = "🐪";

function getLength(str) {
  return [...new Intl.Segmenter().segment(str)].length;
}

console.log(getLength(str1));    // → 1
console.log(getLength(str2));    // → 1
console.log(getLength(str3));    // → 1
```

Recall from the previous recipe that charAt() cannot handle supplementary characters. Let's take advantage of Intl.Segmenter() to write a function that remedies this shortcoming:

part_1/counting_characters/char_segmenter_ex4.js
```
// charAt() alternative

function getChar(str, index) {
  return [...new Intl.Segmenter().segment(str)][index]["segment"];
}

const str = "财🐪";

getChar(str, 0);    // → 财
getChar(str, 1);    // → 🐪
```

This function is very similar to our first function in this recipe, except that it uses [index]["segment"] rather than .length. The expression [index] gets us the character wrapped in an object, and ["segment"] refers to the property of the object that holds the character.

Use the Intl.Segmenter() constructor whenever you want to get the length of a string that contains Unicode characters. But counting characters isn't the only thing that you can do with Intl.Segmenter(). In the next recipe, we'll look at using the API to count the number of words in a string.

Recipe 19

Counting Words in a String with Intl.Segmenter()

Task

Suppose you have a weblog that allows users to submit articles. You have a requirement that each article should have a minimum word count of 500.

You want to create a function that gives feedback to users about their article's word count. To achieve this, your application needs to determine the number of words in a given text string.

One crude solution to this problem is to split the text string by spaces and count the resulting segments. However, this approach may not work correctly in cases where there are multiple consecutive spaces between words, or when the article is written in a language that doesn't use spaces to separate words, such as Korean or Japanese.

You need a solution that can accurately count the number of words in a text, regardless of the language used.

Solution

Call the Intl.Segmenter() constructor with the granularity option set to word:

```
part_1/counting_words/word_segmenter_ex1.js
const str = "White,    red, and blue.";

function countWords(str, lang) {
  const segments = [...new Intl.Segmenter(lang, {granularity: "word"})
                    .segment(str)];
  return segments.filter(item => item.isWordLike === true).length;
}

countWords(str, "en");    // → 4
```

Success! The countWords() function counts the number of words in str based on a specified language (lang).

Browser Compatibility

 At the time of this writing, Firefox has not implemented Intl.Segmenter() yet.[18] Until browser support is more solid, you can run Intl.Segmenter() on the server side with Node 16 or higher.

Discussion

In the previous recipe, we used the default implementation of Intl.Segmenter(), which splits a string at grapheme cluster (user-perceived character) boundaries. This time, we're setting the granularity to word so that the split occurs at word boundaries.

---

18. https://developer.mozilla.org/en-US/docs/Web/JavaScript/Reference/Global_Objects/Intl/Segmenter#browser_com-patibility

The first argument of Intl.Segmenter() determines the locale, which must be a BCP 47 language tag.[19] In this case, we want to split English words, so we pass "en." Once we get the segments of the string, we should filter those that aren't words. Fortunately, the API makes it easy for us by providing the isWordLike property. The filter effectively removes any non-word segments (such as punctuation or numbers).

Finally, we return the length of the filtered segments array, which represents the total number of word segments in the original string. Now, if we want to count the words in another language, all we need to do is pass the corresponding language tag to the countWords() function. For instance, the following example counts the words in Japanese:

part_1/counting_words/word_segmenter_ex2.js
```js
const str = "アジア・東アジアの中でも東方にあります";

function countWords(str, lang) {
  const segments = [...new Intl.Segmenter(lang, {granularity: "word"})
                    .segment(str)];
  return segments.filter(item => item.isWordLike === true).length;
}

countWords(str, "jp");    // → 8
```

Even though the Japanese language has no whitespace between words, the function is able to distinguish word boundaries.

If you search online for a JavaScript solution to count words, you'll surely come across codes like this:

```js
return str.split(" ").length;
```

This code returns an array of words split by a single space character and counts its length. But if your string has double spaces or trailing spaces, the result would be wrong:

```js
const str = "White, red, and  blue. ";
str.split(" ").length;    // → 5
```

Of course, you can fix this problem by filtering the array like this:

```js
const str = "White, red, and  blue. ";

function countWords(str) {
  return str
    .split(" ")
    .filter(a => {return a != ""})
```

---

19. https://www.iana.org/assignments/language-subtag-registry/language-subtag-registry

```
    .length;
}
countWords(str);     // → 4
```

But this solution would work only for languages that use spaces between words. The beauty of using Intl.Segmenter() is its ability to detect word boundaries in different languages.

Counting the Number of a Specific Word with split()

Task

Suppose you want to add search functionality to your application that provides information on how many times a word has appeared in a text. You can use the includes() method to determine whether the word exists within the string. But it doesn't tell you the frequency of the word's appearance.

You want to create a function that counts the number of a specified word (in this case, "cougar") and returns the total number it finds.

Solution

Divide the string into an array of substrings with the split() method, count the number of items in the array by reading its length property, and return the result:

part_1/counting_a_specific_word/split_ex1.js

```
const str = `Cougar is an adaptable, generalist species, occurring in most
American habitat types. Secretive and largely solitary by nature, the cougar
is properly considered both nocturnal and crepuscular. Primary food sources
are ungulates, particularly deer, but cougars also hunt smaller prey such as
rodents.`;

function countWord(str, word, caseSensitivity) {
  if (caseSensitivity) {
    return str.split(word).length - 1;
  } else {
    return str.toLowerCase().split(word).length - 1;
  }
}

console.log(countWord(str, "cougar", true));    // → 2
console.log(countWord(str, "cougar", false));   // → 3
```

The countWord() function returns the total number of occurrences of the word in the str string.

Discussion

The countWord() function accepts three arguments:

- str: A string containing the text to search for a word

- word: A string representing the word to count in the text

- caseSensitivity: A Boolean value indicating whether the search should be case insensitive

Inside the function, we check the value of caseSensitivity. If it has a value of false, we first convert the string to lowercase with the toLowerCase() method. Then we split the str input string at each occurrence of word and return the number of resulting substrings, which is equal to the number of times word appears in str.

Notice the subtraction at the end of the statement. If we pass a string having one instance of "cougar" to split(), it returns an array with two items. The subtraction is necessary to offset one item and get the correct count:

part_1/counting_a_specific_word/split_ex2.js

```
const str = "The word cougar is borrowed from the Portuguese çuçuarana.";
const word = "cougar";

str.split(word);
// → ["The word ", " is borrowed from the Portuguese çuçuarana."]
```

split() is one of those versatile JavaScript tools that come in handy in so many different situations. In this recipe, we incorporated split() in a function to count the number of occurrences of a specific word. But as you've seen in recipes like Recipe 3, Matching the Beginning or End of a String with startsWith() and endsWith(), on page 5 and Recipe 4, Extracting Lists from Text with slice(), on page 8, you can take advantage of split() to solve other text-processing problems as well.

Recipe 21

Equalizing Incompatible Characters with normalize()

Task

Imagine having a cooking application, and you want to add a feature to sort recipes based on the cooking method. The code you developed performs well in sorting recipes for methods like steaming and grilling. However, when it comes to sautéing, the code fails to recognize certain recipes.

After investigating the problem, you realize that the code sometimes fails to match the word "sautéing" even though the characters appear to be the same:

```
part_1/equalizing_characters/normalize_ex1.js
// Notice the length of the strings

const method = "sautéing";
const keyword = "sautéing";

console.log(method === keyword);   // → false
console.log(method.length);        // → 9
console.log(keyword.length);       // → 8
```

"é" in method has a code point of U+00E9, while "é" in keyword consists of two code points: U+0065 and U+0301. As a result, the strict equality operator (===) considers them unequal.

The difference in the number of code points isn't the only reason why your code may fail. Certain characters have the same length but are encoded using two different code points, which can also cause issues with your code.

For instance, the character "Å" can be encoded either as U+212B ANGSTROM SIGN or as U+00C5 LATIN CAPITAL LETTER A WITH RING ABOVE. These two characters aren't equal in JavaScript unless you normalize them.

Solution

Use the normalize() method to convert the strings to a normalized form before comparing them:

```
// Solution

const method = "sautéing";
const keyword = "sautéing";

function areEqual(str1, str2) {
  return str1.normalize("NFC") === str2.normalize("NFC");
}

areEqual(method, keyword);    // → true
```

This function enables us to determine if two strings are equal, taking into account any differences in their Unicode representation.

Discussion

Characters that can be represented more than one way make text processing more difficult. Fortunately, the Unicode standard provides a text normalization procedure that converts strings into forms that can be compared directly for identity.

Inside the areEqual() function, we use the normalize() method to convert both strings to a normalized form using the Normalization Form Canonical Composition (NFC) algorithm. This algorithm ensures that any Unicode characters with multiple code points are represented in their composed form.

We can pass three other arguments to normalize() which we'll look at shortly. The form to use depends on your program requirements, but NFC is usually a better choice for general text because it's more compatible with characters converted from legacy encodings.

Unless you're one of those poor souls who have to support IE11, you don't need a polyfill here. Happily, all modern browsers support normalize().[20] After the normalization, we use the === operator to compare the two strings and return true if they are equal.

We can normalize a string either based on canonical equivalence or based on compatibility. The argument we pass to normalize() determines the form of Unicode normalization:

- Normalization Form D (NFD): Canonical Decomposition

- Normalization Form C (NFC): Canonical Decomposition, followed by Canonical Composition

---

20. https://caniuse.com/mdn-javascript_builtins_string_normalize

- Normalization Form KD (NFKD): Compatibility Decomposition
- Normalization Form KC (NFKC): Compatibility Decomposition, followed by Canonical Composition

Two characters are *canonically equivalent* when they have different code points but are rendered in the same way, just like "é" in our example. When we say NFC performs canonical composition, that means it merges the code points of the character into a single code point, so "é" consisting of U+0065 and U+0301 becomes "é" made of U+00E9. Canonical decomposition is the opposite process.

Now, if two characters have different appearances and code points but have the same meaning, they are classified as *compatibly equivalent*. Take a look at the following table for the two forms of equivalent sequences:

Canonically equivalent	é ↔ e + ́ U+00E9 U+0065 U+0301 Ç ↔ C + ̧ U+00C7 U+0043 U+0327 ñ ↔ n + ̃ U+00F1 U+006E U+0303
Compatibly equivalent	ſ → s U+017F U+0073 ℍ → H U+210D U+0048 ⑥ → 6 U+2465 U+0036 ｶ → カ U+FF76 U+30AB

When we normalize a string, we're telling the program to select one of these equivalent encodings so that the characters are either all composed or all decomposed. Notice how the arrow on some cells points only to the right. That means we can convert a character to its compatibility decomposition form but not the reverse. So, we should be careful when using this type of conversion: if we lose access to the source text, the original form of characters is lost forever because there's no function to revert your text back to its composed form.

Consider the following code:

```
part_1/equalizing_characters/normalize_ex3.js
const str1 = "\u00E9";              // é
const str2 = "\u0065\u0301";        // é

console.log(str1 === str2);         // → false

// normalize str1
const str1norm = str1.normalize("NFD");    // \u0065\u0301

console.log(str1norm === str2);     // → true
```

In this code, we're replacing any canonical composition in str1 with its decomposed forms. If we pass NFC to normalize(), the method does the opposite:

```
part_1/equalizing_characters/normalize_ex4.js
const str1 = "\u00E9";              // é
const str2 = "\u0065\u0301";        // é

// normalize str2
const str2norm = str2.normalize("NFC");     // \u00E9

console.log(str2norm === str1);     // → true
```

The Default Parameter

If you pass no argument to normalize(), it will use NFC.

There are two forms of compatibility normalization: NFKD and NFKC. Conversion to NFKD works just like NFD. It replaces canonical composites in the string with their decomposed forms. Additionally, it replaces any compatibility composites with their decomposition form.

If the glyph is just a compatible composition of another glyph, then normalizing it with NFD or NFC won't change it. On the other hand, both NFKD and NFKC will replace the glyph with its compatible decomposition form:

```
part_1/equalizing_characters/normalize_ex6.js
const str1 = "⑥";      // \u2465

console.log(str1.normalize("NFD"));     // → ⑥ (\u2465)
console.log(str1.normalize("NFC"));     // → ⑥ (\u2465)
console.log(str1.normalize("NFKD"));    // → 6 (\u0036)
console.log(str1.normalize("NFKC"));    // → 6 (\u0036)

const str2 = "⁶";      // \u2076

console.log(str2.normalize("NFD"));     // → ⁶ (\u2076)
console.log(str2.normalize("NFC"));     // → ⁶ (\u2076)
console.log(str2.normalize("NFKD"));    // → 6 (\u0036)
console.log(str2.normalize("NFKC"));    // → 6 (\u0036)
```

In this code, conversion to NFD or NFC does not affect str1 and str2 because the strings are compatible compositions, not canonical compositions. Interestingly, conversion to both NFKD and NFKC produces the same result because NFKC uses compatibility decomposition as the basis for canonical composition. In this case, the character has no canonical composition form, so it's just converted to compatibility decomposition.

The difference between NFKC and NFKD becomes more apparent when a glyph is a canonical composition of glyphs that are compatible with another glyph. Consider the following code:

```
part_1/equalizing_characters/normalize_ex7.js
const str = "ẛ";       // \u1E9B

console.log(str.normalize("NFD"));     // → ẛ (\u017F\u0307)
console.log(str.normalize("NFC"));     // → ẛ (\u1E9B)

console.log(str.normalize("NFKD"));    // → ṡ (\u0073\u0307)
console.log(str.normalize("NFKC"));    // → ṡ (\u1E61)
```

As we said, NFKC uses compatibility decomposition as the basis for canonical composition. The compatibility decomposition of \u1E9B is \u0073\u0307, and the canonical composition of \u0073\u0307 is \u1E61.

Remember, perform text normalization before storing or processing texts to avoid possible pitfalls. But be careful when using normalization forms KD and KC as they discard formatting distinctions that may be essential to the semantics of the text. Therefore, you shouldn't blindly apply them to arbitrary text. NFC is usually a better choice for general text.

Recipe 22

Copying Text to Clipboard with the Clipboard API

Task

Suppose you have a cooking website that provides recipes for different meals, and you want to provide readers with the option of copying the ingredients of the recipes to their clipboard so that they can create a shopping list. To achieve this, you need to create a button that, when clicked, copies the list of ingredients to the clipboard.

Solution

First, set up your HTML elements. You need a button that triggers a JavaScript code. Remember, your program should not attempt to read or write the user's clipboard without permission. So, creating a button that clearly states it copies data to the clipboard is the first step:

part_1/copying_to_clipboard/clipboard_ex1.html

```html
<!doctype html>
<html lang="en-us">
<head>
  <meta charset="utf-8">
  <meta name="viewport" content="width=device-width, initial-scale=1">
  <script src="clipboard_ex1.js" defer></script>
</head>

<body>
  <ul id="ingredients">
    <li>1 cup olive oil</li>
    <li>4 garlic cloves</li>
    <li>1 tablespoon ground cumin</li>
    <li>1 tablespoon chili powder</li>
    <li>2 cans beans</li>
    <li>1 can crushed tomatoes</li>
  </ul>
  <button id="copyBtn" type="button">Copy Ingredients to Cliboard</button>
</body>

</html>
```

Next, locate the button using getElementById() or querySelector(), and add an event listener to it. As soon as the button is clicked, you want to grab the ingredients list and extract its text:

part_1/copying_to_clipboard/clipboard_ex1.js

```js
document.querySelector("#copyBtn").addEventListener("click", () => {

  // Select the list elements
  const nodeList = document.querySelectorAll("#ingredients li");

  // Create a variable that will hold the text to be sent to clipboard
  let textList = "";

  // Append the text of each li element to textList
  nodeList.forEach(li => {
    textList += `*  ${li.textContent} \n`;
  });

  // Append the current URL to textList
  textList += "View recipe at " + window.location.href;
```

```
  writeToClipboard(textList);
});
```

Now, define the function responsible for writing the list to the clipboard:

```
part_1/copying_to_clipboard/clipboard_ex1.js
function writeToClipboard(text){
  navigator.clipboard.writeText(text).then(() => {
    console.log("Copying to clipboard was successful!");
  }, (err) => {
    console.error("Unable to copy text: ", err);
  });
}
```

The main part of the function is the writeText() property of the Clipboard interface. This property returns a promise, so you need to use a then() to handle its result (alternatively, you can use await).

If your code successfully writes the string to the clipboard, you'll get a fulfilled promise, and the code logs a message to the console. If not, you'll get an error.

Discussion

Besides readText() and writeText(), the clipboard API provides two other methods for reading and writing non-text data, such as images, to the user clipboard: read() and write(). While readText() and writeText() work on all browsers, the support for read() and write() is spotty. So be sure to check browser support before you use them in your projects.[21]

When working with the Clipboard API, you might get an error like this:

```
DOMException: Clipboard write was blocked due to lack of user activation.
```

This error is from the Firefox console and indicates you're attempting to write to the clipboard programmatically, but there hasn't been any user interaction with the page, such as clicking on a button. Errors like this are essential for keeping developers' access to the clipboard in check.

Other important factors to consider when using the clipboard API are as follows:

- You may write text to the clipboard without permission, but to read from it, you always need to get user permission (the browser usually pops up a permission dialogue automatically)

---

21. https://caniuse.com/?search=Clipboard

- You can access the clipboard only if the page is the active browser tab

- The Clipboard API is available only in secure contexts (HTTPS)

Previously, the only way to access the clipboard was through the Web API document.execCommand() method. But because this method is synchronous and blocks the browser when reading/writing large data, browser vendors have deprecated it in favor of the clipboard API.

Use the Clipboard interface to provide a smoother experience for your users when they need to copy code snippets, activation keys, tokens, verification codes, etc., but always be explicit about when and what you store in their clipboard.

Wrapping Up

Anything you want to do with text, JavaScript is up to the job. In the first part of this book, you learned how to handle entangled text using JavaScript's built-in methods. This involved sifting through the data and extracting the relevant information, formatting different data types, handling Unicode characters, and more.

In the second part, you will focus on JavaScript's implementation of regular expressions. You will explore the syntax in detail and examine several examples to understand their application.

CHAPTER 2

Part II: Text Processing with Regular Expressions

JavaScript's built-in string methods are excellent for basic text manipulation tasks. But they may not suffice when you need more advanced functionality, such as validating user inputs. This is where regular expressions (commonly abbreviated as regex) become an essential tool in your JavaScript programming toolkit. Regular expressions provide sophisticated pattern-matching capabilities that you can use for complex text validation.

There are several popular implementations of regular expressions, each with its own unique matching algorithm. The behavior of a particular implementation is referred to as its *flavor*. Regex flavors have distinct syntax and feature sets and varying degrees of compatibility with each other.

In Part II, you'll master JavaScript's regex flavor by working through different recipes. If you're new to writing regex in JavaScript, read through the introductory section to familiarize yourself with implementing the patterns in your code; otherwise, you can jump straight into recipes.

Additionally, you'll want to test your patterns with a modern tool, which we talk about in Appendix 3. So, if you don't yet have a tool in place, take a moment to read through Appendix 3, Testing Regex with Specialized Tools, on page 203, and then select and set up a regex tool. You'll be glad to have the tool, especially when building complicated regular expressions, to help you avoid errors.

Recipe 23

Creating Your First Regular Expression

Before using the recipes in Parts 2 and 3, you need to know how to implement regular expressions in your code. In JavaScript, you have two options for creating regular expressions: you can either use the RegExp() constructor or use the regex literal. When using the literal form, you'll need to enclose the pattern in a pair of forward slash (/) characters, like this:

```
part_2/first_regex/first_regex_ex1.js
const re = /Hello/;
```

This regex pattern is made up of five characters that tell the regex engine to find a direct match for "Hello" in a string. A pattern can be as simple as a single literal character such as "i." If there are multiple occurrences of "i" in a string, it matches the first one.

For example, in the string "If opportunity doesn't knock, build a door," the regex matches the "i" in "opportunity," not "build." It also doesn't match the "I" in "If" because that word uses a capital letter. As you will learn later in this part, you can use flags to configure your regular expression to continue searching after the first match or ignore the letter case.

Let's look at another example:

```
part_2/first_regex/first_regex_ex2.js
const re = /123/;

const str1 = "123";
const str2 = "321";

console.log(re.test(str1));    // → true
console.log(re.test(str2));    // → false
```

When running this code, the regex engine tries to find "1," immediately followed by a "2," and immediately followed by a "3." This pattern exists within the first string, so test() returns true, but although the second string contains the same characters, they're not counted as a match because they're not in the correct order.

JavaScript provides several methods to determine whether a pattern exists in a string. The test() method is the simplest one. It returns true if a match exists in the given string or false if otherwise.

We can get the same result with the RegExp() constructor:

```
part_2/first_regex/first_regex_ex3.js
const re = new RegExp("123");

const str1 = "123";
const str2 = "321";

console.log(re.test(str1));    // → true
console.log(re.test(str2));    // → false
```

Unlike the literal form, the RegExp() constructor allows us to construct a pattern dynamically. For example, we can use it to build a pattern out of the items of an array:

```
part_2/first_regex/first_regex_ex4.js
const str = "Debuggers don't remove bugs. They show them in slow motion.";
const arr = ["bug", "flea", "mite", "midge"];
const re = new RegExp(arr.join("|"));

console.log(re.test(str));    // → true
```

A pipe symbol in a regex pattern works like the logical OR (||) operator in JavaScript. It matches either everything to the left of the symbol or everything to the right. In this case, we have four items in the array, and we're joining them with a pipe, so it's like writing the literal form /bug|flea|mite|midge/. The main difference is that RegExp() lets us build the pattern dynamically.

When to Use a Constructor

Keep in mind that the literal form is always faster than the constructor form. So, use a constructor only when you need to build a pattern dynamically.

Another difference between the two forms is that when using the RegExp constructor, it's necessary to use escape characters for backslashes and quotes. Compare:

```
part_2/first_regex/first_regex_ex5.js
// A RegExp pattern
const re1 = new RegExp("\"\\d");

// The literal version of the above pattern
const re2 = /"\d/;

console.log(re1.test('"3'));    // → true
console.log(re2.test('"3'));    // → true
```

To match a quote character in a regex pattern that is already enclosed in quotes, we need to use an escape character to indicate that the quote character is part of the string, rather than a delimiter for the string. An alternative way to write the same pattern would be to use single quotes for the pattern string: new RegExp('"\\d').

\d is a metacharacter in regex that matches a digit. If we don't escape \d, RegExp() will match a backslash followed by a "d" literally:

part_2/first_regex/first_regex_ex6.js
```
const re1 = new RegExp("\d");

console.log(re1.test("\d"));    // → true
console.log(re1.test("3"));     // → false
```

In literal notation, where the pattern is enclosed in forward slashes, we must use a backslash to escape any forward slashes that appear within the pattern. This is necessary because a forward slash marks the end of the pattern in literal notation, and without escaping, it would be interpreted as such. Compare:

part_2/first_regex/first_regex_ex7.js
```
// A RegExp pattern
const re1 = new RegExp("/");

// The literal version of the above pattern
const re2 = /\//;

console.log(re1.test("/"));     // → true
console.log(re2.test("/"));     // → true
```

Case Sensitivity

 By default, regular expressions are case sensitive. The pattern /abc/ does not match Abc, unless you use a special flag called *ignoreCase* to instruct the engine to ignore any differences in letter case. You'll learn about flags later in this part.

But finding a direct match is not the biggest strength of regular expressions. JavaScript already has the indexOf() method that can do that job just fine. Regular expressions are designed to find more complex patterns, such as /\b(\w+)\s+\1\b/gi, which finds duplicate words.

Now that you understand how to implement regex in JavaScript, you're prepared to work on the recipes in Parts 2 and 3.

Recipe 24

Asserting the Start or End of a String with ^ and $

Task

Suppose you have an input field in your app that allows customers to enter their order number and track their package. You want to ensure the user input is a number before searching it in your database. If you are a bit familiar with regex, you know that to match a digit with regex, you can use \d. And to match one or more digits, you can put a plus sign right after it like this:

```
part_2/caret_and_dollar/cnd_ex1.js
const input = "8751409";

function verifyDigits(input) {
  const re = /\d+/;
  return re.test(input);
}

verifyDigits(input);    // → true
```

This regex matches "8751409" as you intended. But it also matches a string like "123abc" or "abc123abc":

```
part_2/caret_and_dollar/cnd_ex2.js
const input = "abc123abc";

function verifyDigits(input) {
  const re = /\d+/;
  return re.test(input);
}

verifyDigits(input);    // → true
```

So what happened here? Your pattern tells the regex engine to match one or more digits, but it doesn't tell it where. So, it successfully matches the digits in the middle of the string and returns true even though there are other non-matching characters in the string.

What you need is a way to specify the beginning and end of the string in your regex so it won't match other characters.

Solution

Place a caret (^) at the beginning and a dollar symbol ($) at the end of the pattern, like this:

```
part_2/caret_and_dollar/cnd_ex3.js
const digits = "8757409";
const digits_and_letters = "875abc";

function verifyDigits(input) {
  const re = /^\d+$/;
  return re.test(input);
}

console.log(verifyDigits(digits));              // → true
console.log(verifyDigits(digits_and_letters));  // → false
```

The regex now matches the exact phrase you're looking for! The caret (^) asserts the position at the start of the string, and a dollar symbol ($) asserts the position at the end of the string.

Discussion

Don't confuse ^ and $ with startsWith() and endsWith(). ^ and $ are known as zero-width assertions, which means they don't match actual characters, but rather positions in the text. So, the caret symbol in /^Hello$/ doesn't match "H" in the input. Instead, it asserts that no other character comes before the literal characters "Hello."

Similarly, the dollar symbol doesn't match any character, it just ensures that the position is the end of the string. If you want to match specific characters at the beginning or end of a string, you should use JavaScript's startsWith() and endsWith() methods (see Recipe 3, Matching the Beginning or End of a String with startsWith() and endsWith(), on page 5).

The Multiline Flag Changes the Rules

 If you use a multiline flag, $ also matches the point before a line break character, and ^ also matches the point after a line break character. We'll cover the multiline flag in Recipe 41, Forcing ^ and $ to Match at the Start and End of a Line with the m Flag, on page 110.

Use ^ and $ to assert a position at the beginning or end of a string, but be careful when using the multiline flag as it changes how these symbols work.

Regex also comes with a syntax for matching whole words only: \b. This syntax, along with ^ and $, are known as *boundaries*. The next recipe tells you all about the word boundary (\b).

Recipe 25

Looking For Whole Words Only with the Word Boundary (\b)

Task

Say you want to look for the word "green" in a document. You try using the includes() method, but it matches other words containing "green" too, such as "greenhouse" and "evergreen":

part_2/word_boundary/word_boundary_ex1.js
```
const str1 = "We must reduce the emissions of greenhouse gases.";
const str2 = "An evergreen plant has leaves for the whole year.";

str1.includes("green");    // → true
str2.includes("green");    // → true
```

Adding a space around "green" doesn't quite cut it because the word might be followed by a comma, appear before/after a newline character, or come at the beginning/end of a sentence, and so on:

part_2/word_boundary/word_boundary_ex2.js
```
const str = "Blend together yellow and blue paint to make green.";

str.includes(" green ");     // → false
```

You need a solution that matches "green" only if it's a separate word.

Solution

Place a \b before and after "green" in the regex pattern to exclude other words:

part_2/word_boundary/word_boundary_ex3.js
```
const re = /\bgreen\b/;
const str1 = "We must reduce the emissions of greenhouse gases.";
const str2 = "An evergreen plant has leaves for the whole year.";
const str3 = "Blend together yellow and blue paint to make green.";

re.test(str1);    // → false
re.test(str2);    // → false
re.test(str3);    // → true
```

Success! You matched "green" only when it was a separate word and not part of another word. You also were able to find "green" in spite of having punctuation around the word. Let's see how \b works to find whole words.

Discussion

The *metacharacter* \b matches at a position known as the *word boundary*. Simply put, this metacharacter allows you to look for "whole words" only. A position qualifies as a word boundary only if a word character is not followed or preceded by another word character.

Therefore, \b matches before the first character or after the last character of a word. Word characters include a-z, A-Z, 0-9, and underscore. So things like spaces (*green beans*), quotation marks (*"green"*), commas (*green,*), and periods (*green.*) are seen as word boundaries.

What Is a Metacharacter?

 When certain characters are used in regular expressions, they give special meaning to the search syntax. These characters are known as metacharacters (or special characters) and allow you to perform a more advanced matching than just searching for a piece of text. Metacharacters can represent ideas such as locations, quantity, or types of characters.

It's pretty common to need to match only whole words (like black, but not blacksmith) and \b is well-suited to that use, but there's more to word boundaries than you might imagine. Let's dig a bit deeper into using \b.

\bgreen\b would not match "green" in "_green" or "green4," because both underscores and digits are word characters, and there is no *boundary* between a word character and another word character:

part_2/word_boundary/word_boundary_ex4.js
```
const re = /\bgreen\b/;

re.test("_green");    // → false
re.test("green4");    // → false
```

Hyphens, however, *do* qualify as word breaks. So, *green-eyed* would be a match in our example. We humans may see *green-eyed* as a single word, but regex doesn't:

part_2/word_boundary/word_boundary_ex5.js
```
const re = /\bgreen\b/;

re.test("green-eyed");    // → true
```

Same thing with the apostrophe: /\bcan\b/ matches "I can't do it" even though "can't" is a contraction and a word in the English sense:

```
part_2/word_boundary/word_boundary_ex6.js
const re = /\bcan\b/;

re.test("I can't do it");     // → true
```

Accented characters are also considered word breaks (for a workaround, see Recipe 53, Matching Unicode Word Boundaries with the Unicode Property Escape, on page 139):

```
part_2/word_boundary/word_boundary_ex7.js
const re = /\bFianc\b/;

re.test("Fiancée");     // → true
re.test("Fiancee");     // → false
```

You don't have to put a pair of \b around words. You can use a single \b to match only one boundary:

```
part_2/word_boundary/word_boundary_ex8.js
const re1 = /\bgreen/;
const re2 = /green\b/;

re1.test("evergreen");     // → false
re1.test("greenhouse");    // → true

re2.test("evergreen");     // → true
re2.test("greenhouse");    // → false
```

Notice that when you place \b at the start of the search string (/\bgreen/) it finds only words that start with "green" and when placed at the end (/green\b/) only words that end with "green."

Using \B for Non-word Boundaries

\B matches any position that \b does not (any non-word boundary) and so we say that \B is the negated form of \b. In regex, it's a normal convention: lower-case and uppercase versions of the same letter being the opposite/negated forms of each other.

\B matches a position where a character is followed or preceded by the same type of character, such as between two space characters or two letters. Here is an example:

```
part_2/word_boundary/word_boundary_ex9.js
const re = /green\B/;

re.test("greenhouse");     // → true
re.test("green bay");      // → false
```

In "greenhouse," "green" is followed by the same type of character: a word character. So, the test returns true. In "green bay," however, "green" is followed by a space (a different type), and so the result is false.

\b with the RegExp Constructor

When using the RegExp constructor, you must escape the \b metacharacter with a backslash because you're writing the pattern in a normal string, not a slash-enclosed literal.

```
new RegExp("green\\B").test("greenhouse");    // → true
```

Using Intl.Segmenter() Instead

Remember Intl.Segmenter() from Recipe 19, Counting Words in a String with Intl.Segmenter(), on page 48? If you're looking for a pure JavaScript solution, you can achieve the same result with Intl.Segmenter():

```
part_2/word_boundary/word_boundary_ex10.js
function includesWord(str, word) {
  let s = [...new Intl.Segmenter("en", {granularity: "word"}).segment(str)];
  return s.some(value => {
    return value.segment === word;
  });
}

includesWord("Her flashing green eyes.", "green");
// → true

includesWord("We must reduce the emissions of greenhouse gases.", "green");
// → false

includesWord("The green-eyed monster", "green");
// → true

includesWord("I can't do it", "can");
// → false
```

When you set the granularity to word, Intl.Segmenter() splits the string at word boundaries. You can then check the items of the resulting array for the word you are looking for with some(), which returns true if at least one element in the array matches the word. One difference between this approach and our regex solution is how it handles the apostrophe: \b treats an apostrophe as a word break while Intl.Segmenter() does not.

Another difference is that the Intl.Segmenter() approach is slower than regex, especially if you're testing a large block of text. So, unless you want to avoid matching words that have an apostrophe, you should stick with regex.

Use the word boundary (\b) when looking for "whole words" in a string, but be wary of accented characters, hyphens, and apostrophes since they qualify as word breaks. And use the negated version of the word boundary (non-word boundary \B) to match a position that \b does not.

Recipe 26

Matching One of Several Alternatives with the Vertical Bar (|)

Task

Imagine you want to match specific variations of the word "week," including "weekend" and "weekly," but not "weekday." You want the match to be at word boundaries, so other words like "Newsweek" wouldn't count as a match. What you need is a way to define alternative patterns in the regex.

Solution

Use a vertical bar (|) to form an alternation. The vertical bar character will tell the regex engine to match any one of a series of patterns:

```
part_2/vertical_bar/vertical_bar_ex1.js
const re = /\bweek\b|\bweekend\b|\bweekly\b/;

re.test("How much do you earn per week?");          // → true
re.test("Employees are paid weekly.");              // → true
re.test("The office is closed on the weekend.");    // → true
re.test("Your story could be featured on Newsweek!"); // → false
```

The regex engine matches everything left of the vertical bar or everything right. The pattern in this example has three alternatives, each enclosed in a pair of word boundaries. So, it will only match "week," "weekend," or "weekly."

Discussion

If you want to add other symbols to the pattern but don't want them to be a part of the alternation, you can use parentheses. Using parentheses will limit the scope of the alternation.

Remember, a vertical bar matches either everything to the left or everything to the right. So, if you wanted to match "this week" or "this weekend," you could write /\bthis (week|weekend)\b/:

part_2/vertical_bar/vertical_bar_ex2.js
```
const re = /\bthis (week|weekend)\b/;

re.test("Are you free this weekend?");    // → true
re.test("Are you free this week?");        // → true
re.test("weekend");                        // → false
```

This pattern tells the regex engine to find a word boundary, then "this" followed by a space, then either "week" or "weekend," and then another word boundary.

You could also use parentheses to rewrite the solution in this recipe in a more compact form:

part_2/vertical_bar/vertical_bar_ex3.js
```
const re = /\b(week|weekend|weekly)\b/;

re.test("How much do you earn per week?");          // → true
re.test("Employees are paid weekly.");              // → true
re.test("The office is closed on the weekend.");    // → true
re.test("Your story could be featured on Newsweek!"); // → false
```

The outcome is identical, but the pattern is more readable. Since all three alternatives in this example begin with the same word, we can further fine-tune the regular expression engine by rephrasing the regex as follows:

part_2/vertical_bar/vertical_bar_ex4.js
```
const re = /\bweek(end|ly|)\b/;

re.test("How much do you earn per week?");          // → true
re.test("Employees are paid weekly.");              // → true
re.test("The office is closed on the weekend.");    // → true
re.test("Your story could be featured on Newsweek!"); // → false
```

The options in parentheses tell the regex engine to match "end," "ly," or nothing. The empty option at the end of the parentheses is necessary to be able to match "week." Alternatively, you could use a quantifier to make the pattern in the parentheses optional, like this: /\bweek(end|ly)?\b/, which is more conventional (see Recipe 29, Repeating Part of a Regex with Quantifiers, on page 80).

Regex engines typically match words in a list from left to right. Therefore, arranging words with the highest probability of appearing in the text at the beginning of the list might slightly enhance the engine's performance.

Remember, take advantage of alternation when you want to match one of a choice of regular expressions, and add parentheses to limit the scope of the alternation.

Recipe 27

Matching One of Several Characters with the Character Class

Task

Suppose you want to find a word in a document even if it is misspelled. For example, the word "license" is one of the most misspelled words in English. You want to write a pattern that matches "license," "licence," "lisence," or "lisense" in a document.

Solution

Use a character class:

```
part_2/character_class/character_class_ex1.js
const re = /li[sc]en[sc]e/;

re.test("A driver's license");   // → true
re.test("A driver's lisense");   // → true
re.test("A driver's licence");   // → true
re.test("A shopping list");      // → false
```

A character class matches only one out of the specified characters. In this code, the specified characters are "s" and "c," so the regex matches "license," "licence," "lisense," or "lisence," but not "liscense." Keep in mind that a character class matches only one character.

Discussion

Certain characters change the behavior of the character class. If you place a caret (^) after the opening square bracket, it negates the entire character class. That means the character class will match any character that isn't one of the specified characters.

So, /[^license]/ would match any character that isn't "l," "i," "c," "n," "s," and "e":

```
part_2/character_class/character_class_ex2.js
const re = /[^license]/;

re.test("lie");    // → false
re.test("list");   // → true
```

This pattern matches "t" in "list," so test() returns true. You might have noticed that the caret (^) is the same as the one that matches the beginning of a string (Recipe 24, Asserting the Start or End of a String with ^ and $, on page 65). Although the character is the same, its meaning is entirely different.

It's just like the English word "arm" can mean different things depending on what context it is used in (sometimes a part of the body, sometimes to provide a weapon).

Also, keep in mind that caret has a special meaning only when used right after the opening bracket of the character class. So, /[a^bc]/ wouldn't negate the character class because "^" would be treated as a literal character.

As with a regular class, a negated class must match a character to be successful. For example, the pattern /Number[^5]/ matches "Number6" but not "Number" because the class expects a character:

```
part_2/character_class/character_class_ex3.js
const re = /Number[^5]/;

re.test("Number6");    // → true
re.test("Number");     // → false
```

Use a character class to match a character out of several characters, such as when you want to consider misspelled words or spelling differences in American and British English.

Use a negated character class to list characters you don't want to appear in a string. An exciting aspect of the character class is its ability to match a range of characters, which you'll learn about in the next recipe.

Recipe 28

Matching a Range of Characters with Character Classes

Task

Suppose you're tasked with searching scanned documents and filtering applicants aged between 20 and 40. The info you need to extract is preceded with "age:". So, your regex pattern should match the word "age," followed by a colon, followed by a space, and followed by a range of numbers between 20 and 40.

With what you've learned so far, you could use vertical bars in a pair of parentheses to specify the possible matches, like this:

part_2/character_class_range/range_ex1.js
```
/Age: (2(0|1|2|3|4|5|6|7|8|9)|3(0|1|2|3|4|5|6|7|8|9)|40)/
```

But what would you do if you wanted to look for a larger range of numbers? You need a better way of defining the range of characters in regex.

Solution

Use a character class and place a hyphen between the range of numbers you're looking for:

part_2/character_class_range/range_ex2_v1.js
```
const re = /Age: (2[0-9]|3[0-9]|40)/;

re.test("Name: John | Age: 23");    // → true
re.test("Name: Ana | Age: 54");     // → false
```

When a hyphen appears within a character class, it's treated as a metacharacter. But there's an exception: if it's the first or last character in the class, it can't possibly define a range, so it loses its special meaning and is considered a normal character.

You can even further shrink the pattern like this:

part_2/character_class_range/range_ex2_v2.js
```
const re = /Age: ([23][0-9]|40)/;

re.test("Name: John | Age: 23");    // → true
re.test("Name: Ana | Age: 54");     // → false
```

Here, [23] matches 2 or 3, and [0-9] matches a single digit in the range of 0 to 9. Together, they match a number between 20 to 39. The vertical bar at the end tells the engine to either match 20-39 or 40.

Discussion

If your regex involves only verifying a range of digits, you can achieve the same result with JavaScript's built-in methods. Consider the following example:

part_2/character_class_range/range_pure_js.js
```
const str1 = "Name: John | Age: 23";
const str2 = "Name: Ana | Age: 54";

function verifyAge(str) {
  const index = str.indexOf("Age: ");
  const endIndex = index + 5;
  const age = str.slice(endIndex, endIndex + 2);
```

```
  if (age >= 20 && age <= 40) {
    return true;
  } else {
    return false;
  }
}
console.log(verifyAge(str1));    // → true
console.log(verifyAge(str2));    // → false
```

This code performs the following steps:

- It finds the index of Age: in the input string

- It adds the length of the substring Age: to the index to get the position of the digits

- It extracts the digits using the slice() method

- It then checks if the extracted age is within a valid range using the less than or equal (<=) and greater than or equal (>=) operators

Letting JavaScript determine whether a digit is in the range is often less error-prone. A common mistake among regex learners is to define double-digit ranges with a single-character class. The pattern [12-24] doesn't match a number between 12 and 24. Instead, it matches a "1," "2," or "4" (equivalent to [124]).

Here's how the regex engine interprets [12-24]:

- 1 matches the character "1"
- 2-2 matches a single character in the range between "2" and "2"
- 4 matches the character "4"

To define a pattern that matches a double-digit range, we'll need to use two character classes and a vertical bar:

part_2/character_class_range/range_ex3_v1.js
```
const re = /1[2-9]|2[0-4]/;

re.test("10");     // → false
re.test("15");     // → true
re.test("24");     // → true
re.test("25");     // → false
re.test("015");    // → true
re.test("240");    // → true
```

Is there anything missing in this pattern? Yes, a pair of word boundaries (\b). Without word boundaries, the pattern would also match "015" and "150." So, to match a double-digit range between 12 and 24, our pattern should look like this:

```
part_2/character_class_range/range_ex3_v2.js
const re = /\b1[2-9]|2[0-4]\b/;

re.test("10");     // → false
re.test("15");     // → true
re.test("24");     // → true
re.test("25");     // → false
re.test("015");    // → false
re.test("240");    // → false
```

The range we define with a hyphen isn't limited to digits. We can define a range of alphabets, too. For example, [a-z] matches any lowercase letter, and [A-Z] matches any uppercase letter:

```
part_2/character_class_range/range_ex4_v1.js
const re = /Group [A-Z]/;

re.test("Group B");     // → true
re.test("Group 2");     // → false
```

We can even list multiple ranges, like this:

```
part_2/character_class_range/range_ex4_v2.js
const re = /Group [A-Z0-9]/;

re.test("Group B");     // → true
re.test("Group 2");     // → true
```

The order in which we specify the ranges doesn't matter. So, [A-Z0-9] is the same as [0-9A-Z]. To list the range of characters we don't want to be included, we can apply a caret (^). If we use /Group [^A-C]/, the class matches "Group" followed by a space followed by a character that's not "A," "B," or "C":

```
part_2/character_class_range/range_ex5.js
const re = /Group [^A-C]/;

re.test("Group A");     // → false
re.test("Group B");     // → false
re.test("Group C");     // → false
re.test("Group D");     // → true
re.test("Group 5");     // → true
```

Using Predefined Ranges

Matching a range of characters is one of the most common tasks in regular expressions. For this reason, regex flavors offer special characters as shorthands for matching character ranges. Most shorthands comprise a backslash and a character like \d, which matches a digit character. The full stop (.) is an exception. It's the only shorthand character class that isn't preceded by a backslash.

Keep the following list of shorthand character classes bookmarked—they are bound to come in handy.

Digit Character (\d)

\d matches any ASCII digit character, which is equivalent to [0-9]. For example:

part_2/character_class_range/range_ex6.js
```
const re = /\d/;

re.test("5");     // → true
re.test("a");     // → false
```

Word Character (\w)

\w matches any ASCII word characters, which is the same as [A-Za-z0-9_]. Keep in mind that the underscore is a word character in regex:

part_2/character_class_range/range_ex7.js
```
const re = /\w/;

re.test("5");     // → true
re.test("a");     // → true
re.test("_");     // → true
re.test("*");     // → false
```

Space Character (\s)

\s matches any Unicode whitespace character. For instance:

part_2/character_class_range/range_ex8.js
```
const re = /\s/;

re.test("5");     // → false
re.test(" ");     // → true
```

As you'll see later in this book, an interesting use of \s is to remove duplicate whitespaces from a string (see Recipe 62, Removing Duplicate Whitespaces, on page 162).

Non-Digit Character (\D)

\D matches any character that isn't a digit, which is the same as [^\d] or [^0-9]:

part_2/character_class_range/range_ex9.js
```
const re = /\D/;

re.test("5");     // → false
re.test("a");     // → true
re.test(" ");     // → true
```

Negated Shorthands

\D, \W, and \S are the negated forms of \d, \w, and \s respectively. That means they match the opposite of what normal shorthand character classes match.

Non-Word Character (\W)

\W matches any character that isn't a word character. Short for [^\w] and [^A-Za-z0-9_]:

part_2/character_class_range/range_ex10.js
```
const re = /\W/;

re.test("5");      // → false
re.test("a");      // → false
re.test(" ");      // → true
re.test("*");      // → true
```

Non-Space Character (\S)

\S matches any character other than whitespace. Short for [^\s]:

part_2/character_class_range/range_ex11.js
```
const re = /\S/;

re.test("5");      // → true
re.test("a");      // → true
re.test(" ");      // → false
re.test("*");      // → true
```

Where Can You Use Shorthands?

Shorthands may appear both inside and outside square brackets. For instance, while \s\d matches a whitespace character followed by a digit character, [\s\d] matches either a single whitespace character or a single digit character.

Single Character (.)

A full stop (.) matches any single character except for a line break. For example:

part_2/character_class_range/range_ex12.js
```
const re = /./;

re.test("5");      // → true
re.test(" ");      // → true
re.test("*");      // → true
re.test("abc");    // → true
```

Notice the last test that returns true for "abc." Here, the full stop matches "a" in "abc," not the entire string. To match three consecutive characters, you can use the regex /.../. Alternatively, you can use /.{3}/, which takes advantage of a quantifier to specify the number of tokens to match. You'll learn about quantifiers in Recipe 29, Repeating Part of a Regex with Quantifiers, on page 80.

Be careful when matching characters that span multiple lines. A full stop won't match a line break character unless you use a special flag (see Recipe 42, Forcing . to Match Newline Characters with the s Flag, on page 113).

You can use a character class to define a range of characters to match. The range can be specified using a hyphen (-), and it's not limited to numbers. To match a character that is not in a specific range, use the caret (^) immediately after the opening bracket. To specify ranges using a more compact syntax, you can take advantage of predefined character classes.

Recipe 29

Repeating Part of a Regex with Quantifiers

Task

Suppose you want to add an option to your program that allows users to log in with a PIN code. The main benefit of using a PIN instead of a password is faster login. I tend to put my computer to sleep when I'm away, even for a short time. Conveniently, my OS lets me log in quickly with only a PIN code.

Say you want to implement a similar feature for your application. You need to write a regex pattern that 1) validates the input is digits and 2) ensures the number of digits is between 4 and 6 characters.

Solution

Place a pair of curly brackets after the \d character class to specify how many times the digits should occur:

part_2/quantifiers/quantifiers_ex1.js
```
const re = /^\d{4,6}$/;

re.test("107");       // → false
re.test("1077");      // → true
re.test("107781");    // → true
re.test("1077815");   // → false
```

The pattern {n,m} lets us match the preceding item at least n times and at most m times (n and m must be positive integers).

The regex in this code begins with a caret (^) and ends with a dollar symbol ($). We don't want to match anything other than a 4-6 digit input, so we delimit the pattern with ^ and $ (for further explanation of how caret and dollar work, see Recipe 24, Asserting the Start or End of a String with ^ and $, on page 65).

Without $, this pattern would match a string like "107781pass":

```
part_2/quantifiers/quantifiers_ex2.js
/\d{4,6}/.test("107781pass");    // → true
```

Discussion

We can match a token or group repeatedly using a quantifier. {4} is a quantifier that tells the regex engine to match its preceding item precisely four times. So, the pattern [0-5]{4} is equivalent to [0-5][0-5][0-5][0-5], but is easier to read and write.

If we use a quantifier to repeat a character class, the entire character class will be repeated, not just the character it matches. For example, the pattern [car]{3} matches three consecutive characters made of "c," "a," and "r":

```
part_2/quantifiers/quantifiers_ex3.js
const re = /[car]{3}/;

re.test("car");      // → true
re.test("arc");      // → true
re.test("carbon");   // → true (matches the first three characters)
```

To repeat the same character matched by a character class, we can use a backreference (discussed later in Recipe 46, Referencing a Matched String with the Backreference, on page 123).

A character class is the only place in regex where quantifiers don't have a special meaning. For example, /[c{3}]/ matches a single character that's a "c," "{", "3", or "}". To take away the special meaning of a quantifier outside a character class, we must escape it with a backslash. For instance:

```
part_2/quantifiers/quantifiers_ex4.js
const re = /\{7\}/;

re.test("{7}");    // → true
re.test("7");      // → false
re.test("abc");    // → false
```

In this pattern, \{ matches the character { literally. Without a backslash, { would indicate the beginning of a quantifier.

Although curly brackets are a common type of quantifier used in regex, there are other quantifiers available as well. The following section provides information about these additional quantifiers.

Types of Quantifiers

Quantifiers specify the number of occurrences of a character, group, or character class to match. There are six forms of quantifiers in regex: zero or more (*), one or more (+), zero or one (?), exactly n times {n}, at least n times {n,}, and from n to m times {n,m}. Let's look at each and how you might use them.

Zero or More (*)

An asterisk matches zero or more sequences of the preceding item. Let's say we want to match all verb forms of the word "play," including "played," "plays," and "playing." By using a quantifier after the character class (\w), we can tell regex to match "play" and any character that might come after it as long as it's a word character:

```
part_2/quantifiers/quantifiers_ex5.js
const re = /\bplay\w*\b/;

re.test("He plays for Cleveland");              // → true
re.test("France is playing England tomorrow."); // → true
re.test("Evans played very well.");             // → true
re.test("Let's play a different game");         // → true
```

Note that this pattern also matches words like "playful" and "playground." To limit the match to a set of specific words, we can use a vertical bar (see Recipe 26, Matching One of Several Alternatives with the Vertical Bar (|), on page 71).

One or More (+)

A plus sign matches one or more sequences of the preceding item. For example, the regular expression /Go+al/ attempts to match the letter G followed by one or more instances of the letter o, followed by the letters a and l:

```
part_2/quantifiers/quantifiers_ex6.js
const re = /Go+al!/;

re.test("Goooooooooal!");   // → true
re.test("Goal!");           // → true
re.test("Gal!");            // → false (expects at least one instance of o)
```

Zero or One (?)

A question mark matches zero or one occurrence of the preceding item. For example, if we wanted to match the word "apple" or its plural form, "apples," we'd write \apples?\. This pattern tells the regex engine to match the word "apple" followed by zero or one instance of the letter "s":

```
part_2/quantifiers/quantifiers_ex7.js
const re = /apples?/;

re.test("An apple a day keeps the doctor away");    // → true
re.test("Peel and core the apples");                // → true
```

Exactly n Times {n}

Specifies how often the preceding item can be repeated. n must be a positive integer. For example, we can use /\b\w{3}\b/ to match any three-letter word in a string:

```
part_2/quantifiers/quantifiers_ex8.js
const re = /\b\w{3}\b/;

re.test("A car accident.");     // → true
re.test("A driver's license");  // → false
```

From n to m Times {n,m}

Matches the preceding item at least n times and at most m times. n and m must be positive integers. We have already seen this pattern in action. But, let's take a look at another example to better understand how it works:

```
part_2/quantifiers/quantifiers_ex10.js
const re = /\bim{1,2}\w*?/;

re.test("immaculate");    // → true
re.test("impact");        // → true
re.test("insane");        // → false
```

Here, the pattern attempts to match a word boundary, followed by the letter "i," followed by one or two instances of the letter "m." As a result, it matches any word that begins with "im" or "imm."

At Least n Times {n,}

{n,} is similar to {n,m} in that it matches the preceding item at least n times, but it doesn't have a second parameter. For example, the regular expression /\d{2,}/ matches two or more digits:

```
part_2/quantifiers/quantifiers_ex9.js
const re = /\d{2,}/;

re.test("1");      // → false
re.test("12");     // → true
re.test("123");    // → true
```

Similar Quantifiers

The pattern {1,} is equivalent to the quantifier +, {0,} is equivalent to *, and {0,1} is equivalent to ?.

Use quantifiers to specify the numbers of characters or expressions to match. Different types of quantifiers let you precisely set how many times the preceding item should be matched.

Recipe 30

Treating Multiple Characters as a Single Unit with the Capturing Group

Task

Suppose you want to search an archive of documents and retrieve those that mention a date in August. The only clue you have is that the date comes in four different styles. For example: "August 16," "August 16th," "Aug 16," or "Aug 16th."

To match such a date with regex, you need a way to make "ust" in "August" and "th" in "16th" optional.

Solution

To make certain letters optional, group them by enclosing them in parentheses and place a question mark after the group:

```
part_2/capturing_group_p1/capturing_group_p1_ex1.js
const re = /\bAug(ust)?\s\d{1,2}(st|nd|rd|th)?\b/;

// Grouping allows matching many alternatives
re.test("Aug 16");         // → true
re.test("August 16");      // → true
re.test("Aug 16th");       // → true
re.test("August 16th");    // → true
```

This regex matches dates in the format of "Aug 1st," "August 15th," "Aug 22nd," "August 31st," etc. Please note that if the date contains typographical errors such as "August 16nd" or "Aug 1rd," the pattern will still match them.

Discussion

Let's start by examining the pattern step by step:

```
/\bAug(ust)?\s\d{1,2}(st|nd|rd|th)?\b/
```

- \b asserts a word boundary
- Aug matches the characters Aug literally
- (ust)? 1st capturing group
  - ust matches the characters ust literally
  - ? matches the previous token zero or one time
- \s matches any whitespace character
- \d matches a digit
  - {1,2} matches the previous token 1 or 2 times
- (st|nd|rd|th)?
  - 1st alternative st: matches the characters st literally
  - 2nd alternative nd: matches the characters nd literally
  - 3rd alternative rd: matches the characters rd literally
  - 4th alternative th: matches the characters th literally
  - ? matches the previous token zero or one time
- \b asserts a word boundary

The regex begins with a word boundary (\b), which allows us to match the beginning of a word. Then we use Aug(ust)? to match the string "Aug" followed by an optional "ust," which tells the regex to match both "Aug" and "August" formats of the month. After that, we use \s to match a whitespace character (space, tab, etc.) after the month.

For the day of the month, we use \d{1,2} to match one or two digits. The curly braces with the range 1,2 ensure that only one or two digits are matched. Next, we use (st|nd|rd|th)? to match the suffix for the day of the month, including "st," "nd," "rd," or "th." Of all metacharacters, the vertical bar has the lowest precedence: it matches either everything to the left or everything to the right of the vertical bar. In this case, we need to limit the reach of alternation by wrapping the characters in a pair of parentheses.

Then we use a question mark to make the suffix optional. Finally, we end the regex with a word boundary (\b) to match the end of a word.

Don't Use the Capturing Group in a Character Class

It's not possible to use the capturing group in a character class because parentheses inside a character class are treated as literal characters. For example, [x(y)] matches a single character out of x, (, y, and).

Sometimes it's useful to group a part of the regular expression and treat it as a single unit. You can do this by encapsulating the characters in parentheses. Grouping enables you to use quantifiers on the entire group, limit alternation to only a part of the pattern, or extract a matched value for further processing (which is the topic of our next recipe).

Recipe 31

Extracting a Matched Value with the Capturing Group

Task

Suppose you need to search for a file with a .pdf extension and extract only the filename without the extension. Typically, regular expressions return the entire matched string, but you want a solution that enables you to identify and extract a specific part of the matched string for further processing.

Solution

Place a pair of parentheses around the specific part of the pattern that you want to extract:

```
part_2/capturing_group_p2/capturing_group_p2_ex1.js
const re = /\b(\w+)\.pdf\b/;
const str = "Please download data_p2x53.pdf";

const result = str.match(re);

if (result) {
  console.log(result[1])
} else {
  console.error("No match found.");
}
// Logs:
// → data_p2x53
```

You can now access the filename by referencing the second item of the resulting array.

Discussion

In this example, we used the match() method instead of test(). Unlike test(), which gives a yes/no as an answer (a Boolean value) indicating whether or not a match is found, match() provides more detailed information in the form of an array. We can access the substring captured by the capturing group in the regex using the second element of the resulting array (result[1]). Since JavaScript arrays are zero-indexed, the second element is available at index 1.

Pay attention to the type of value that match() is called on. Unlike test(), which is a property of the RegEx object, match() is a property of the String object and so must be called on a string.

Now, let's examine the regex:

```
/\b(\w+)\.pdf\b/
```

- \b asserts the position at a word boundary
- (\w+) 1st capturing group
  - \w matches any word character
  - + matches the previous token one or more times
- \. matches the period character . literally
- pdf matches the characters pdf literally
- \b asserts a word boundary

The regex pattern starts with a word boundary (\b), which means the match must occur at the beginning of a word. Next, we use (\w+) to match one or more word characters. The parentheses around \w+ signal that this group should be captured and made available for further use.

After that, we use .pdf to match the literal characters ".pdf," and once again use \b to match a word boundary, ensuring the ".pdf" is at the end of a word. Putting it all together, this regex matches any word that ends with ".pdf" characters.

Parentheses are a versatile tool in regex. They not only let us group tokens and apply quantifiers to them but also enable us to extract matched values for further processing. But the meaning of parentheses can change if we place special characters right after the opening bracket. The next recipe explains more.

Recipe 32

Excluding Groups from Result with the Non-capturing Group

Task

Let's say you need to keep track of a particular golf player's ranking based on information scraped from the player's profile on a sports blog. The ranking information is in a string with an ordinal indicator such as "3rd" or "4th." You only care about the number, not its suffix, and want to use a capturing group to extract it for additional processing.

If you use /(\d{1,2})(st|nd|rd|th)/, the second parentheses will capture the suffix, too, which is redundant. You need a way to tell the regex engine not to capture those letters.

Solution

Add a question mark (?) and a colon (:) right after the opening parentheses to create a *non-capturing group*:

part_2/non_capturing_group/non_capturing_ex1.js
```
const re = /(\d{1,3})(?:st|nd|rd|th)/;
const str = "Tiger Woods sits 16th in the latest World Golf Ranking.";

const match = str.match(re);

if (match) {
  console.log("Player Rank: " + match[1]);     // → Player Rank: 16
}
```

Your regex is now able to match the ordinal number "16th," and you can access the number in the second item of the resulting array.

Discussion

The pattern in this recipe matches an ordinal number but remembers only the first capturing group: the digits. The second group is *non-capturing* because there's a question mark and a colon right after the opening parentheses.

So, unlike the capturing group, it doesn't capture anything from the substring it matches. Here, "16th" is the string we want to match, "16" is the substring we want to capture, and "th" is the substring we want to exclude.

Let's take a closer look at the pattern:

/(\d{1,3})(?:st|nd|rd|th)/

- (\d{1,3}) 1st capturing group
  - \d matches a digit (equivalent to [0-9])
  - {1,3} matches the previous token between 1 to 3 times
- (?:st|nd|rd|th) non-capturing group
  - 1st Alternative: st matches the characters st literally
  - 2nd Alternative: nd matches the characters nd literally
  - 3rd Alternative: rd matches the characters rd literally
  - 4th Alternative: th matches the characters th literally

The match() method returns a wealth of information about the result. In this case, we're interested in only the second item of the array, which is the ranking number without the ordinal indicator, so we use str.match(re)[1].

A non-capturing group may have a quantifier like a regular group. In the following example, the final question mark makes the group optional, so the pattern matches non-ordinal numbers as well:

part_2/non_capturing_group/non_capturing_ex2.js
```
const re = /(\d{1,3})(?:st|nd|rd|th)?/;
const str = "Tiger Woods sits 16 in the latest World Golf Ranking.";

const match = str.match(re);

if (match) {
  console.log("Player Rank: " + match[1]);    // → Player Rank: 16
}
```

The question mark at the end of this regex is not related to the one in the group. It simply tells the regular expression engine to match zero or one occurrence of the group.

Remember, to avoid capturing a matched substring, use a non-capturing group instead of a regular one. Your code may also benefit from using non-capturing groups when adding more groupings to an existing pattern. This way, you won't have to make major changes when revising a pattern. There's also a minor performance improvement in some engines because JavaScript doesn't have to add the group to the result.

Recipe 33

Reading Groups with Ease Using Named Capturing Groups

Task

Suppose you need to find the exact time when an error occurred by searching through a log file. You know that the time is in the format of hours, minutes, seconds, and AM/PM indicator (HH:MM:SS XM). To extract each time segment, you create a pattern that can recognize and capture each segment separately. However, as the number of groups in the pattern increases, the already cryptic regex syntax becomes even harder to read. Consider this example:

```
part_2/named_capturing_group/ncg_ex1.js
const re = /(\d{2}):(\d{2}):(\d{2})\s(\w{2})/;
const match = "09:30:00 AM".match(re);

console.log(match[1]);
console.log(match[2]);
console.log(match[3]);
console.log(match[4]);
```

Which one of these matches represents minutes? And which one represents seconds? Using a more expressive syntax to group the segments can greatly reduce the chances of encountering issues in your code.

Solution

Use named capturing groups:

```
part_2/named_capturing_group/ncg_ex2.js
const re = /(?<hour>\d{2}):(?<min>\d{2}):(?<sec>\d{2})\s(?<period>\w{2})/;
const match = "09:30:00 AM".match(re);

console.log(match.groups.hour);      // → 09
console.log(match.groups.min);       // → 30
console.log(match.groups.sec);       // → 00
console.log(match.groups.period);    // → AM
```

A named capturing group uses a more extended syntax in the form of (?<name>...). So, patterns with multiple capturing groups can be read and edited with less difficulty.

Discussion

Named capturing groups is a syntax introduced in ES2018. A valid capturing group name must be an alphanumeric sequence starting with a letter. To avoid name collision with existing property names, JavaScript assigns all named groups to a separate object called groups.

If a pattern has an optional named capturing group that does not participate in the match, it will still create a property for that group on the groups object. Let's make the last capturing group in our code optional by placing a question mark after it to see what happens:

```
part_2/named_capturing_group/ncg_ex3.js
const re = /(?<hour>\d{2}):(?<min>\d{2}):(?<sec>\d{2})\s?(?<period>\w{2})?/;

// A timestamp without AM/PM
const str = "09:30:00";

const match = str.match(re);
```

```
console.log(match.groups);
// → {hour: "09", min: "30", sec: "00", period: undefined}
```

In this example, period doesn't participate in the match, but it's still included in the groups object. Even if there is no named group in the regex, the groups object will be available in the result:

part_2/named_capturing_group/ncg_ex4.js
```
const re = /\w+/;
const match = "abc".match(re);

console.log("groups" in match);     // → true
```

It's also possible to use numbered references to access named groups. Of course, employing numbered references would defeat the purpose of our recipe (reading the value of groups with ease). However, you may find numbered references useful when you want to improve the readability of the regex part of your code only:

part_2/named_capturing_group/ncg_ex5.js
```
const re = /(?<hour>\d{2}):(?<minute>\d{2}):(?<second>\d{2})/;
const match = "09:30:00".match(re);

console.log(match[0]);    // → 09:30:00
console.log(match[1]);    // → 09
console.log(match[2]);    // → 30
console.log(match[3]);    // → 00
```

Take advantage of the named capturing group syntax when writing patterns with multiple capturing groups to easily edit the pattern and read the result.

Recipe 34

Using Special Replacement Patterns

Task

Imagine you have a private group web page where members agreed to share their contact information with other members. You don't want to impose any restrictions on the phone number format the website accepts other than it should consist of ten digits. So, a user might enter 123-456-7890, 123 456 7890, or (123)4567890.

But you want to transform the digits into a formatted phone number so they will display consistently, like (123) 456-7890, throughout the website. To achieve this, you first need to remove any existing formatting from the number and then format it the way you want.

Solution

Remove all formatting by replacing non-digit characters with an empty string:

part_2/replacement_patterns/replacement_ex1_p1.js
```
const phoneNum = "123-456-7890";
const re = /\D/g;

phoneNum.replace(re,"");     // → "1234567890"
```

To format the number, use capturing groups to match different sections of the phone number, and refer to each section with a replacement pattern:

part_2/replacement_patterns/replacement_ex1_p2.js
```
const phoneNum = "1234567890";
const re = /(\d{3})(\d{3})(\d{4})/;

phoneNum.replace(re, "($1) $2-$3");     // → "(123) 456-7890"
```

Your final code should look like this:

part_2/replacement_patterns/replacement_ex1_final.js
```
const phoneNum = "123-456-7890";

function formatPhoneNumber(num) {

  // Remove non-digits
  num = num.replace(/\D/g,"");

  // Format the number
  num = num.replace(/(\d{3})(\d{3})(\d{4})/,
                  "($1) $2-$3");

  return num;
}

formatPhoneNumber(phoneNum);     // → "(123) 456-7890"
```

Success: you now have a nicely formatted phone number to display despite a variety of formats entered by users.

Discussion

In this recipe, we use the replace() method to execute the regex patterns. replace() takes a regex as its first argument, attempts to find a match in the given string, and replaces it with its second argument. The first regex consists of only one metacharacter: \D, which matches any non-digit character. When we use it with the global flag (g), we get a string with all non-digit characters removed.

The second regex formats the number. When we use capturing groups, input strings that match are stored in memory and available to be recalled later. In this case, we're recalling the first, second, and third capturing groups by using *special replacement patterns* in the form of $1, $2, and $3, respectively.

A special replacement pattern starts with a dollar sign and has a special meaning when used in the second argument of the replace() method. The result is a formatted phone number ready to be displayed to the end user.

Exploring Other Special Replacement Characters

Besides $n, other special characters exist that allow reusing the portions of the matched text. These characters are the only special constructs accepted in a replacement string, so metacharacters like \w aren't valid. Similarly, special replacement characters only work in the replacement string and have no special meaning in a regex pattern.

$<Name>

Includes a named capturing group. Here's an example of what the solution in this recipe would look like if we wrote it with named capturing groups:

```
part_2/replacement_patterns/replacement_ex3.js
const phoneNum = "123-456-7890";

function formatPhoneNumber(num) {

  // Remove non-digits
  num = num.replace(/\D/g,"");

  // Format the number
  num = num.replace(/(?<area>\d{3})(?<exchange>\d{3})(?<line>\d{4})/,
                 "($<area>) $<exchange>-$<line>");

  return num;
}

formatPhoneNumber(phoneNum);    // → "(123) 456-7890"
```

For further explanation of named capturing groups, see Recipe 33, Reading Groups with Ease Using Named Capturing Groups, on page 89.

$n

Includes the nth captured group, where n is a positive integer. You've already seen this special character in action, but we're including it here for comparison:

```
part_2/replacement_patterns/replacement_ex7.js
const str = "cold & hot";
const re = /(cold)\s&\s(hot)/;

str.replace(re, "$2 & $1");     // → "hot & cold"
```

Available Only in Regex

> $n and $<Name> constructs have a special meaning only if the pattern is a regex. In a string, they're treated as literals.

$&

Includes a copy of the matched substring. For example:

```
part_2/replacement_patterns/replacement_ex4.js
const str = "FAT is a computer file system architecture";
const re = /FAT/;

str.replace(re, "$& (File Allocation Table)");
// → "FAT (File Allocation Table) is a computer file system architecture"
```

$'

A dollar sign followed by an apostrophe includes the portion of the input that comes after the matched substring. For instance:

```
part_2/replacement_patterns/replacement_ex5.js
const str = "#3";
const re = /#/;

str.replace(re, "#$'");     // → "#33"
```

$'

A dollar sign followed by a backtick includes the portion of the input that comes before the matched substring:

```
part_2/replacement_patterns/replacement_ex6.js
const str = "1000 liter";
const re = /liter/;

str.replace(re, "liter = $`kg");     // → "1000 Liter = 1000 kg"
```

Sometimes the difference between an apostrophe and a backtick can be hard to see. A way to remember the difference is that the backtick points backward and so gives you the string that comes before the match.

$$

Includes a dollar sign ($):

```
part_2/replacement_patterns/replacement_ex8.js
const str = "€700";
const re = /€/;

str.replace(re, "$$");     // → "$700"
```

We'll talk about this pattern in more detail in Recipe 35, Taking Away the Special Meaning of Replacement Patterns, on page 95.

Ordering

You may use special replacement characters more than once and in any order.

Take advantage of special replacement characters inside a replacement string to reference different parts of the matched substring. One thing to remember about replace() is that it does not modify the original string. Instead, it creates a new string, performs the replacement operation, and returns the edited copy.

Recipe 35

Taking Away the Special Meaning of Replacement Patterns

Task

Suppose your task is to add the pricing for different services to a website's blog. More specifically, you need to add the fee for tire replacement at a car service center. In your first attempt, you come up with a solution like this:

```
part_2/neutralizing_replacement/nrp_ex1.js
const str = "In our shops, tire change takes about 15 minutes.";
const re = /\b(tire change)\b/;

str.replace(re, "$1 (which cost $10 for each tire)");
// → "In our shops, tire change (which cost tire change0 for each tire)
// takes about 15 minutes."
```

This regex attempts to find the phrase "tire change" in a string and add the cost in parentheses. It uses a special replacement pattern in the form of $1, but because the regex treats $10 as a special replacement pattern, the result is unusable.

You need a solution to take away the special meaning of $1 in $10, which has a corresponding capturing group in the pattern, and use the characters literally.

Solution

Escape the dollar sign with another dollar sign:

part_2/neutralizing_replacement/nrp_ex2.js
```
const str = "In our shops, tire change takes about 15 minutes.";
const re = /\b(tire change)\b/;

str.replace(re, "$1 (which cost $$10 for each tire)");
// → "In our shops, tire change (which cost $10 for each tire) takes
// about 15 minutes."
```

Successful outcome! The dollar sign neutralizes the special meaning of $1, so the regex engine recognizes it as literal characters.

Discussion

In this recipe, the regex has a single capturing group. But, what happens if you try to refer to a group that doesn't actually exist? If you type $2 in the replacement text, it won't correspond to anything. For example:

part_2/neutralizing_replacement/nrp_ex3.js
```
const str = "In our shops, tire change takes about 15 minutes.";
const re = /\b(tire change)\b/;

str.replace(re, "$1 (which cost $20 for each tire)");
// → "In our shops, tire change (which cost $20 for each tire) takes
// about 15 minutes."
```

If you use a two-digit reference in the replacement string, the outcome will depend on the number of capturing groups in the pattern. If you have ten capturing groups and use $10, it refers to the tenth capturing group. If you have fewer capturing groups, $10 only uses the first digit that refers to the first capturing group and uses 0 as a literal replacement string. This is what happened in the first example in this recipe: "$1" in "cost $10" referenced "tire change" and "0" was treated as a literal character.

The takeaway from this recipe is to use $ to neutralize the special meaning of a replacement pattern.

Recipe 36

Using a Function as the Replacement Pattern

Task

Suppose your task is to improve an online real-estate marketplace that lists property specifications in square feet. You need to write a code that finds square feet values and provides a square meter version in parentheses so that international buyers can easily understand them.

Solution

Start with creating a function that converts a square feet value to a square meter (m2):

```
function convertToM2(sqft) {

  // remove non-digit characters
  sqft = sqft.replace(/\D/g, "");

  // convert sqft to m2
  const m2 = sqft * 0.0929;

  // round to two decimal places and return it
  return m2.toFixed(2);
}
```

Now, you need a function that receives a string as input and scans it for digits followed by units such as "sqft," "sq. ft," or "sq ft." Once a match is found, you want to call the convertToM2() function to convert the value into square meters, and then append the converted result to the original matched value.

That's where using a function as the replacement argument comes in:

```
function appendM2ToSqft(str) {
  return str.replace(/\d+,?\d+\s(sqft|sq\.?\sft)/ig, (match) => {
    return `${match} (${convertToM2(match)} m2)`;
  });
}
```

Here's how the final code looks like:

```
part_2/replacement_fn/replacement_fn_ex1.js
const str = "3 Beds, 2.5 baths, 1,850 Sq. Ft";

// Convert sqft to m2
function convertToM2(sqft) {
```

```
  // Remove non-digit characters
  sqft = sqft.replace(/\D/g, "");

  // Convert sqft to m2
  const m2 = sqft * 0.0929;

  // Round to two decimal places and return it
  return m2.toFixed(2);
}

// Match sqft in the string, have it converted to m2,
// wrap parentheses around the result, and append it to sqft
function appendM2ToSqft(str) {
  return str.replace(/\d+,?\d+\s(sqft|sq\.?\sft)/ig, (match) => {
    return `${match} (${convertToM2(match)} m2)`;
  });
}

appendM2ToSqft(str);
// → "3 Beds, 2.5 baths, 1,850 Sq. Ft (171.86 m2)"
```

Using this code, you can list the size of a property in both square feet and square meters.

Discussion

Let's start with examining the regex pattern:

`/\d+,?\d+\s(sqft|sq\.?\sft)/ig`

- \d matches a digit
  - ○ + matches the previous token between one and unlimited times
- , matches the character "," literally
  - ○ ? matches the previous token zero or one time
- \d matches a digit
  - ○ + matches the previous token between one and unlimited times
- \s matches any whitespace character
- (sqft|sq.? ft) 1st capturing group
  - ○ sqft 1st alternative
    - ○ sqft matches the characters "sqft" literally
  - ○ sq\.?\sft 2nd alternative
    - ○ sq matches the characters "sq" literally
    - ○ \. matches a period literally
      - ○ ? matches the previous token zero or one time
    - ○ \s matches any whitespace character
    - ○ ft matches the characters "ft" literally
- Flags
  - ○ i enables case-insensitive matching
  - ○ g enables global matching, which indicates we want to look for all matches, rather than stopping after the first match

The replace() method accepts either a string or a function as the replacement argument. If you use a function, it gets executed for every match, and its output becomes the replacement text.

The replacement function has the following syntax:

```
part_2/replacement_fn/replacement_fn_ex2.js
function replacer(match, p1, p2, /* …, */ pN, offset, string, groups) {
  return replacement;
}
```

The first parameter contains the matched string (similar to $&). If there are capturing groups, they will be available next to the first parameter (p1, p2, /* …, */ pN).

The next parameter provides the offset of the matched string. So, if you had "Hello" as a string and "ll" as a search pattern, the offset would be 3. There's also a string parameter containing the entire supplied string.

Finally, the groups parameter will be available if you have at least one named capturing group in the pattern. In this recipe, we're only using the first parameter, so we leave out other parameters.

Inside the replacer function, we use a template literal to get the value of match and pass it to the convertToM2() function. convertToM2() first strips the string of non-digit characters by replacing them with an empty string. Then it performs the conversion and returns the result. The outcome is a string containing a square meter value in parentheses that's appended to the original matched string.

Take advantage of a replacement function when you need to perform calculations or process the matched value in the replacement string.

Recipe 37

Escaping Metacharacters with the Backslash

Task

Suppose you have an array of quotations that uses square brackets to include words within a quote that are not part of the original quote:

```
const quotes = [
  "The children [Hansel and Gretel] found a house made of candy.",
  "Fortune favors the bold.",
  "They [France] are playing against England tomorrow.",
  "Everything you've ever wanted is on the other side of fear.",
  // ...
]
```

You want to find those instances containing square brackets so that you can add them to a new collection for search purposes:

```
const quotesWithMod = [
  "The children [Hansel and Gretel] found a house made of candy.",
  "They [France] are playing against England tomorrow.",
]
```

Since a bracket has a special meaning in regex, you need a way to escape the bracket character to match the actual bracket.

Solution

Precede the brackets with a backslash (\) to match for the actual bracket:

part_2/backslash/backslash_ex1.js

```
Line 1   const quotes = [
           "The children [Hansel and Gretel] found a house made of candy.",
           "Fortune favors the bold.",
           "They [France] are playing against England tomorrow.",
     5     "Everything you've ever wanted is on the other side of fear.",
           // ...
         ]

         const quotesWithMod = [];
    10   const re = /\[\w+(?:\s\w+)*\]/;

         quotes.forEach(quote => {
           if (re.test(quote)) {
             quotesWithMod.push(quote);
    15     }
         });

         console.log(quotesWithMod);

    20   // log:
         // [
         //    "The children [Hansel and Gretel] found a house made of candy.",
         //    "They [France] are playing against England tomorrow."
         // ]
```

You now have a separate array containing quotes with words that are not part of the original quote.

Discussion

The regex in our example matches any text enclosed in square brackets, which could contain one or more words separated by spaces. Pay attention to the backslash character preceding [and]. Without a backslash, these brackets would be treated as a character class. \w and \s are different: the backslash before them is a part of the expression and creates a shorthand character class (see Recipe 28, Matching a Range of Characters with Character Classes, on page 74).

When a backslash is followed by certain characters, it has a special meaning in the regular expression. For example, \n will represent a line feed, and \s will match a whitespace character. But we can also use a backslash to escape metacharacters. When we want to take away the special meaning of a metacharacter and use it as a literal character, we need to precede it with a backslash. For instance, to match a backslash followed by the letter "s," we write \\s.

Let's look at the regex pattern step by step:

```
/\[\w+(?:\s\w+)*\]/
```

- \[matches the character "[" literally
- \w matches a word character (ASCII letter, digit, or underscore)
  - + matches the previous token between one and unlimited times
- (?:\s\w+)* non-capturing group
  - (?: indicates the start of a non-capturing group
  - \s matches a whitespace character
  - \w matches a single word character (ASCII letter, digit, or underscore)
    - + matches the previous token between one and unlimited times
  -) closes the non-capturing group
  - * matches the previous token between zero and unlimited times
- \] matches the character "]" literally

In line 12, we try to loop through each quote in the quotes array using the forEach() method. Inside the loop, we call the test() method on the regex to check whether the current quote contains a word enclosed in square brackets. If the test returns true, we add the current quote to the quotesWithMod array using the push() method.

In the end, the quotesWithMod array will contain all the quotes from the quotes array that include a word enclosed in square brackets.

Escaping a Normal Character

If you attempt to escape a character that is not a metacharacter, the character will be treated as a literal character and nothing will happen to it. In other words, escaping a non-metacharacter will not have any effect on the character's interpretation by the engine. Here's an example:

```
/\g/.test("g");    // → true
```

But there is one exception to this rule: if you set the u flag, the engine will enforce stricter rules about the unnecessary use of backslashes and throw an error. For more on the u flag see Recipe 43, Enabling Unicode Features with the u Flag, on page 116.

Remember, you can use a backslash when you want to take away the special meaning of a metacharacter and use it as a literal character in a regex pattern.

Recipe 38

Creating Lazy Quantifiers with the Question Mark

Task

Suppose your task is to write a script that reduces the size of HTML files by removing all comments. The syntax for an HTML comment is <!-- Comment -->. So, to accomplish this task, you might assume that you just need to remove the opening and closing brackets of the comment syntax and any characters that exist between them:

```
part_2/lazy_quantifiers/lazy_ex1.js
const re = /<!--.*-->/;
const str = "HTML comment: <!-- I'm a comment -->";

str.replace(re, "");    // → "HTML comment: "
```

Here, the full stop (.) matches any character (except for a line break), and the quantifier * tells the engine to do this zero or more times. This pattern works for a single-line comment. What about comments that span multiple lines?

Since the full stop (.) doesn't match line break characters, the regex will fail. A common workaround is to use a character class, like [\d\D], in place of a full stop. \d matches any digit character, and \D matches everything else. Combined, they let you match any character:

```
part_2/lazy_quantifiers/lazy_ex2.js
const re = /<!--[\d\D]*-->/;
const str = `HTML comment: <!--
I'm a comment
-->`;

str.replace(re, "");    // → "HTML comment: "
```

But your code should be able to remove all comments, not just one. So, add a g flag at the end of the regex:

```
part_2/lazy_quantifiers/lazy_ex3.js
const re = /<!--[\d\D]*-->/g;
const str = `HTML comment: <!-- I'm a comment -->
Another comment: <!--
I'm a comment
-->`;

str.replace(re, "");    // → "HTML comment: "
```

The g flag tells the regular expression engine to search the entire string for all matches of the pattern, instead of stopping at the first match.

Now you have another problem! The pattern matches the opening bracket of the first comment and everything that comes after it till the closing bracket of the last comment. The reason is that quantifiers—in this case *—are greedy! They try to match as many occurrences of the preceding token as possible, which isn't what you want to get this task done.

You need a way to change how a quantifier behaves.

Solution

Make the * quantifier lazy by placing a question mark after it:

```
part_2/lazy_quantifiers/lazy_ex4.js
const re = /<!--[\d\D]*?-->/g;
const str = `HTML comment: <!-- I'm a comment -->
Another comment: <!--
I'm a comment
-->`;

str.replace(re, "");
// → "HTML comment:
// Another comment: "
```

Your regex is now able to match each comment precisely.

Discussion

As you learned in Recipe 29, Repeating Part of a Regex with Quantifiers, on page 80, the + quantifier allows you to match the preceding token one or more times. So, the pattern \w+ matches one or more word characters in a string.

But in a string like "str," should \w+ match "s" or "str"? How does the regex engine decide between matching "one" or "more" characters? Quantifiers are greedy by default, matching the previous token as many times as possible. A question mark forces the quantifier to take the opposite approach (non-greedy) and match as few times as possible. Compare:

```
part_2/lazy_quantifiers/lazy_ex5.js
const str = "str";

str.match(/\w+?/)[0];     // → "s"
str.match(/\w+/)[0];      // → "str"
```

The pattern [\d\D]*? in this recipe matches zero or more occurrences of any character (including digits and non-digits) while trying to match as few characters as possible. The result is matching the first occurrence of --> rather than the last.

Nicknames for Laziness

 A lazy quantifier is also known as non-greedy or reluctant.

Possessive Quantifiers

JavaScript doesn't support possessive quantifiers. A possessive quantifier is similar to a greedy one but offers better performance in certain situations.

Keep in mind that using a question mark immediately after a quantifier, including *, +, ?, or {}, makes the quantifier lazy.

Recipe 39

Global and Case-Insensitive Matching with the g and i Flags

Task

Suppose your task is creating a U.S. version of an existing company website. You need to search the content of web pages, find instances of the word "tyre," including its plural form "tyres," and replace each with its American spelling "tire." The search must ignore the letter case, so it matches "Tyre" at the beginning of sentences as well.

Another requirement is to find all possible matches in the string. So, rather than stopping the search as soon as a match is found, the engine must continue looking for more matches in the rest of the string. Doing all these manually takes a lot of time. Fortunately, regex *flags* are here to save the day.

One More Time?

You have already seen the i and g flags in action in the previous recipes. This recipe looks at them one more time to solidify your understanding of them.

Solution

Place i and g at the end of the pattern:

part_2/flag_global_insensitive/gi_ex1.js
```js
const str = `Tyre pressure is expressed as pounds per square inch
(PSI). Proper tyre pressure is necessary for optimal handling.
It's important to inspect your tyres every month for wear.`;

const re = /\b(t)yre(s)?\b/gi;

str.replace(re, "$1ire$2");
// → "Tire pressure is expressed as pounds per square inch (PSI).
// Proper tire pressure is necessary for optimal handling. It's important
// to inspect your tires every month for wear."
```

Mission accomplished! All instances of "tyre" in the string are replaced with "tire."

Discussion

In regex literals, it's possible to specify options by adding single-letter flags, also known as modifiers, following the forward slash that terminates the pattern. Normally, the replace() method replaces only the first occurrence of the specified pattern in a string. But here, we're using the global search flag (g), which instructs the engine to continue searching for other pattern occurrences.

The i flag complements the g flag by asking the engine to perform the match in a case-insensitive manner. Here's how each token in this regex works:

```
/\b(t)yre(s)?\b/gi
```

- \b asserts the position at a word boundary
- (t) 1st capturing group
  ○ t matches the character "t" literally
- yre matches the characters "yre" literally
- (s)? 2nd capturing group
  ○ s matches the character "s" literally
  ○ ? matches the previous token between zero or one time (greedy)
- \b asserts the position at a word boundary
- Flags
  ○ g global match
  ○ i case-insensitive match

Pay attention to the special characters $1 and $2 in the second argument of replace(). These characters have special meanings when used in the replacement string. The pattern $n includes the value matched by the nth captured group.

Here, $1 refers to the character matched by the first capturing group, and $2 refers to the character matched by the second capturing group. So, if the pattern matches the word "Tyre" with a capital "T," that specific word will be replaced with "Tire."

Similarly, if the pattern matches the optional "s" in the word "tyres," that word will be replaced with "tires." To learn more about special replacement patterns, see Recipe 34, Using Special Replacement Patterns, on page 91.

JavaScript's regular expression flavor supports seven optional flags, including d, g, i, m, s, u, and y. Similar to g, these flags are placed after the closing delimiter in the literal form, or passed as the second argument to the RegExp() constructor. We'll look at each of these flags in the recipes that follow.

Recipe 40

Generating Indices for Matches with the d Flag

Task

Suppose you're building a tool that helps detect errors and potential problems in JavaScript code. You need your tool to be able to detect the use of reserved words in variables and functions and warn the user.

Ideally, you want to program your tool to pinpoint the exact part of the code where the reserved word is misused rather than outputting just a line number. So, if the code has a variable assignment with a reserved word like this:

```
let default = 7;
```

You want to indicate the error like this:

```
let default = 7;
    ↑------ Invalid variable name
```

To achieve this task, you need a regex that provides the start and end indices of the match.

Solution

Send the supplied code one line at a time to a function that looks for an invalid variable/function name. Use the d flag to obtain the start and end indices of the name:

part_2/flag_indices/indices_ex1.js
```
// The js code you want to check.
// In production, you'll likely use the FileReader API
// or a textarea to grab the code.
const code = `
  let a = 123;
  let b = 456;
  let default = 7;
`;

// A short list of js reserved words.
// A full list is available here:
// https://mzl.la/3XG92DO
const reserved = ["class", "default", "this", "case", "if"];
```

```
// Build a regex pattern with the reserved words
const re = new RegExp(`(?:var|let|const|function)\\s+(${reserved.join("|")})`,
                      "d");

// Find and display the location of the reserved word
function locateReservedWord(line) {
  const match = line.match(re);

  // If no match is found, return
  if (match === null) {return;}

  // Assign the start and end indices using the destructuring assignment.
  // indices[0] holds the indices of the matched string.
  // indices[1] holds the indices of the first capturing group.
  const [start, end] = match.indices[1];

  // Build the error message
  const error =
    " ".repeat(start) +     // Add spaces before the arrow
    "↑" +
    "-".repeat(end - start - 1) +
    " Invalid name (reserved word)";

  console.log(line);
  console.log(error);
}

// Split the code into separate lines,
// then send each line to locateReservedWord()
code.split(/\n|\r|\r\n/).forEach(line => {
  locateReservedWord(line);
});

// Logs:
// → let default = 7;
// →     ↑------ Invalid name (reserved word)
```

Your code can now indicate the exact position of a reserved word in a variable or function name.

Browser Compatibility

Despite being a newcomer to the regex family, the d Flag is supported by all modern browsers.[1] In the Node environment, you'll need a minimum version of 16.0.0 (Released 2021-04-20). To support older browsers, you can use a polyfill available in the regexp-match-indices package on NPM.[2]

---

1. https://mzl.la/3u78Y6w
2. https://www.npmjs.com/package/regexp-match-indices

Discussion

The hasIndices flag (d) indicates that the matching result should provide additional information about the start and end positions of each matched substring. The information will be stored in a property named indices. Consider this example:

part_2/flag_indices/indices_ex2.js
```
const str = "word1 word2";
const re = /word/dg;

console.log(re.exec(str).indices[0]);    // → [ 0, 4 ]
console.log(re.exec(str).indices[0]);    // → [ 6, 10 ]
```

When we set the d flag in a regex, an indices property will be available in the result of exec(), match(), and matchAll(). Here, we're using the exec() method, which is similar to match() except that it provides indices in the global mode too (see Appendix 2, Implementing Regex in JavaScript, on page 195).

The regex in this recipe requires using the RegExp() constructor because we're constructing the pattern dynamically with an array of reserved words. Any backslash in RegExp() must be escaped with another backslash. So, we write the shorthand character class to match whitespaces in the form of \\s rather than \s. Remember, if your dynamically created list contains a backslash, you must escape it too.

Also, pay attention to the second parameter of RegExp(). The RegExp() constructor uses a different approach to set the flags: it takes an optional second parameter containing the letters of the flags to set. Here, we want to set the hasIndices flag, so we pass d. As with the first argument, the second argument must be a string. Do not wrap it in slashes.

Let's analyze the regex in more detail:

```
(?:var|let|const|function)\\s+(${reserved.join("|")})
```

- (?:var|let|const|function) non-capturing group
  ○ 1st alternative: matches the characters "var" literally
  ○ 2nd alternative: matches the characters "let" literally
  ○ 3rd alternative: matches the characters "const" literally
  ○ 4th alternative: matches the characters "function" literally
- \\s matches any whitespace character
  ○ + matches the previous token between one and unlimited times
- (${reserved.join("|")}) 1st Capturing Group
  ○ ${reserved.join("|")} retrieves the array of reserved words and joins its items with a vertical bar, resulting in class|default|this|case|if
- Flags
  ○ d provides information about the start and end indices

Take advantage of the hasIndices flag to obtain information about the start and end positions of matches. Remember, when using the RegExp() constructor, you can't append flags to the regex pattern the way you typically do with regex literals. Instead, you should pass a string containing the flags as the second argument of the constructor.

Recipe 41

Forcing ^ and $ to Match at the Start and End of a Line with the m Flag

Task

Imagine you have a database of movie subtitles and want to provide a search mechanism that returns complete lines containing a specific word. You have already seen how to assert the start and end of a string in Recipe 24, Asserting the Start or End of a String with ^ and $, on page 65.

But this time, you want to assert the start and end of a line. So, if the search word is "McClaren" and the subtitle file contains these lines:

```
...

491
00:39:21,396 --> 00:39:23,481
Soon as you can, get that plane ready.

492
00:39:23,565 --> 00:39:27,485
Dr. McClaren could lose his leg
without proper medical attention.

...
```

You want to retrieve only the line containing "McClaren":

```
Dr. McClaren could lose his leg
```

Solution

To retrieve a complete line, place a caret (^) at the beginning and a dollar symbol ($) at the end of your regex pattern. Then enable the multiline mode by setting the m flag:

```
part_2/flag_multiline/multiline_ex1.js
const re = /^.*\bMcClaren\b.*$/m;
const str = `
491
00:39:21,396 --> 00:39:23,481
Soon as you can, get that plane ready.

492
00:39:23,565 --> 00:39:27,485
Dr. McClaren could lose his leg
without proper medical attention.
`;

str.match(re)[0];
// → "Dr. McClaren could lose his leg"
```

With the m flag, your regex is able to match the line of text containing the word "McClaren."

Reading the File from a Server

Ideally, you'll want to read a subtitle from your server, and a useful tool for that job is the fetch() method.[3]

Discussion

The multiline flag allows the regex engine to process a string consisting of multiple lines. By default, caret (^) and dollar ($) assert the beginning and end of a string, but in multiline mode, they match the beginning and end of a line (delimited by non-printable characters like \n and \r). Compare:

```
part_2/flag_multiline/multiline_ex2.js
const str = `
Anderson
Miller
McClaren
`;

const re1 = /^McClaren$/;
const re2 = /^McClaren$/m;

re1.test(str);    // → false
re2.test(str);    // → true
```

---

3.   https://developer.mozilla.org/en-US/docs/Web/API/fetch

In this string, there's a non-printable newline character at the end of each word, which indicates the end of a line of text and the start of a new one. You can confirm that by searching for the escape sequence (\n) in the string:

part_2/flag_multiline/multiline_ex3.js

```
const str = `
Anderson
Miller
McClaren
`;

const re = /Anderson\n/;

re.test(str);      // → true
```

What Is a Non-printable Character?

A non-printable character (also known as a control character) doesn't represent a written symbol. Instead, it tells certain applications, such as web browsers, how a document is supposed to look. Non-printable characters are designed to indicate formatting actions such as horizontal tab, line feed, carriage return, etc.

Let's dig a bit deeper into the regex pattern:

```
/^.*\bMcClaren\b.*$/m;
```

- ^ asserts the position at the start of a line
- . matches any character
  - ○ * matches the previous token between zero and unlimited times
- \b asserts the position at a word boundary
- McClaren matches the characters "McClaren" literally
- \b asserts the position at a word boundary
- . matches any character
  - ○ * matches the previous token between zero and unlimited times
- $ asserts the position at the end of a line
- Flags
  - ○ m enables multiline mode

The most important thing to remember from this recipe is to use the multiline flag (m) when you want to change the default behavior of the caret (^) and the dollar symbol ($) to match the beginning and end of a line.

Recipe 42

Forcing . to Match Newline Characters with the s Flag

Task

Suppose you want to write a script that removes all comments from JavaScript files to reduce their file size. Removing single-line comments is easy: just find a line that starts with double forward slashes and delete the entire line.

But removing block comments with the /* */ syntax that may span multiple lines is a bit trickier. You might expect a pattern like /\/*.**\// to work because it finds a /* followed by any character until it reaches */.

But, the full stop token in this pattern won't match line break characters, so the regex could fail:

```
part_2/flag_dotall/dotall_ex1.js
const re = /\/\*.*?\*\//;

const comment = `/* this
is a multiline
comment */`;

re.test(comment);    // → false
```

An old workaround is to use two opposite shorthand character classes, such as [\w\W]. Since all characters are either word characters or non-word characters, the character class will match any character, including \r and \n:

Fortunately, ES2018 introduced the dotAll mode that fixes this problem more elegantly.

Solution

Append the s flag to the end of your pattern like this:

```
part_2/flag_dotall/dotall_ex2.js
const re = /\/\*.*?\*\//s;

const comment = `/* this
is a multiline
comment */`;

re.test(comment);    // → true
```

Your regex now can match block comments that span multiple lines of text. Now, let's take advantage of this feature to build a function that takes a string and removes all JavaScript comments from it:

```
part_2/flag_dotall/dotall_ex3.js
// Remove js comments
function removeComments(str) {

  // Match block comments (/*...*/)
  const re1 = /\/\*.*?\*\//sg;

  // Match single line comments (//...)
  const re2 = /\/\/\s.+/g;

  // Remove comments
  let code = str.replace(re1, "");
      code = code.replace(re2, "");

  return code;
}

const jsCode =
`// a variable
let abc = 123;
/* another
variable */
let def = 456;`;

console.log(removeComments(jsCode));
//
// let abc = 123;
//
// let def = 456;
```

Note that in some cases, this solution might not be able to remove JavaScript comments accurately. For example, double forward slashes (//) enclosed in a string is not a comment anymore, but regex doesn't see them that way and removes them. Or */ in the middle of a block comment doesn't end the comment in the eye of the JavaScript interpreter, but that's not the case with regex. To strip comments from JavaScript more accurately, you can take advantage of an AST parser, such as acorn.[4]

Discussion

The beauty of using a flag to change how the full stop works is that it lets us activate the mode on a per-regex basis. This way, existing regular expression patterns that rely on the old behavior of the full stop won't be affected.

---

4.   https://github.com/acornjs/acorn

In this recipe, we created a function that removes both single-line and block JavaScript comments from a given string. To avoid overcomplicating the regex, we used two different patterns to match each type of comment separately. After finding all matches, we replaced them with an empty string, and returned the modified string.

The first pattern matches a multiline comment that starts with /* and ends with */. Since forward slashes are also used to delimit regular expressions in JavaScript, we need to escape it with a backslash to match a literal forward slash. Similarly, we need to escape the asterisk with a backslash to match a literal asterisk:

```
/\/\*.*?\*\//sg
```

- \/ matches the character / literally
- * matches the character * literally
- . matches any character
  - *? matches the previous token between zero and unlimited times, as few times as possible (lazy)
- * matches the character * literally
- \/ matches the character / literally
- Flags
  - s: enables matching newline characters
  - g: enables searching for all matches

We use .*? to match any sequence of characters, including line breaks, but as few as possible. The ? makes the * lazy. This is important because we want to match only the content of the comment and not any subsequent comments.

Next, we use *\/ to match a literal asterisk followed by a forward slash. The s flag at the end of the pattern enables the "dot all" mode. Without this flag, the . wouldn't match line breaks, and the regex wouldn't match multiline comments.

The second regex matches any sequence of characters that begins with two forward slashes ("//") followed by a whitespace character, and then followed by one or more of any character except a newline character. We need to escape each forward slash by adding a backslash before it:

```
/\/\/\s.+/g
```

- \/ matches the character / literally
- \/ matches the character / literally
- \s matches any whitespace character
- . matches any character
  - + matches the previous token between one and unlimited times, as many times as possible (greedy)
- Flags
  - g: enables searching for all matches

We use ".+" to match everything until the end of the line. It's not necessary to add any extra expression to make the matching stop at the end of the line. Just be sure that the s flag is not set for this regex.

The full stop is perhaps the most commonly used metacharacter in the regular expression. By default, it matches any single character except for line-break characters. But more often than not, we want to match line breaks, too. The dotAll mode offers a simple remedy to this problem that can be activated by the s flag.

Recipe 43

Enabling Unicode Features with the u Flag

Task

Suppose you have an online forum and want to limit the characters in user posts to words, numbers, underscores, hyphens, and emoticons. You can impose the first four rules with a character class like [-\w]+. Recall from Recipe 27, Matching One of Several Characters with the Character Class, on page 73 that \w is equivalent to [a-zA-Z0-9_], so you just need to add the hyphen and emoticons.

Matching emoticons is a bit more complicated. In Unicode, emoticons are a block of code points containing 80 Unicode emojis. But adding all these code points to your character class would be a real chore.

You need a solution that enables you to define a range of emojis in the character class, just as you'd define a range of characters.

Solution

List the first and last emojis of the emoticons Unicode block in a character class and place a hyphen between them to define a range.[5] Then, append the u flag to the pattern to enable matching emoji ranges:

part_2/flag_unicode/unicode_ex1.js
```
// Match words, numbers, underscores, hyphens, and emoticons
```

---

5.   https://en.wikipedia.org/wiki/Emoticons_(Unicode_block)

```
const re = /[-\w☺-🙏]+/u;
const str = "123abc-_ 😂😆🐒";

if (re.test(str) === false) {
  throw new Error("Invalid character in post.");
}
```

Your pattern is now able to match a range of emojis successfully!

Discussion

Although the regex in this recipe contains two hyphens, each serves a different purpose. The first hyphen matches a hyphen literally because it is located at the beginning of the character class and cannot possibly define a range. The second hyphen, however, is placed between two emojis, which tells the regex engine to match a range:

/[-\w☺-🙏]+/u

- [-\w☺-🙏] character class: matches a single character in the list below
  - - matches the character - literally
  - \w match any word character
  - ☺-🙏 matches a single character in the range between ☺ and 🙏
- + matches the previous token one or more times
- Flags
  - u: enables unicode features

Without the u flag, this code would throw a SyntaxError:

part_2/flag_unicode/unicode_ex2.js
```
// Same pattern with no unicode flag

const re = /[-\w☺-🙏]+/;
const str = "123abc-_ 😂😆🐒";

if (re.test(str) === false) {
  throw new Error("Invalid character in post.");
}

// → Uncaught SyntaxError: invalid range in character class
```

Another use of the Unicode flag is to tell the engine to treat a pattern as a sequence of Unicode code points, making it possible to interpret surrogate pairs as whole characters rather than two separate characters. For instance:

```
part_2/flag_unicode/unicode_ex3.js
const str = "\ud846";
```

```
/[蠱]/.test(str);          // → true
/[蠱]/u.test(str);         // → false
```

The Chinese character in this example consists of two code points: \ud846\udf10. Without setting the u flag, the regex engine incorrectly interprets the first pair as a match. For more details about Unicode, see Appendix 1, What Is Unicode?, on page 191.

An important thing to remember about the u flag is that it's more strict about the unnecessary use of the backslash. If you escape a character that has no special meaning in regex, and the Unicode mode is on, you'll get an error:

```
part_2/flag_unicode/unicode_ex4.js
const str = "cab";

/\c/.test(str);
// → false

/\c/u.test(str);
// → SyntaxError: Invalid regular expression: /\c/: Invalid Unicode escape
```

The second regex in this code attempts to escape "c," which is not a reserved character. The outcome is a SyntaxError.

Unicode Property Escapes

 An extremely useful feature of the Unicode flag is to enable Unicode property escapes, which you'll learn about in Recipe 51, Matching Non-ASCII Numerals with the Unicode Property Escape, on page 134.

Nitty-Gritty Details

 There are more nitty-gritty details about the u flag that could be useful to know if you are working with non-BPM characters. Check out Mathias Bynens' extensive article on Unicode-aware regular expressions to learn more.[6]

The Unicode flag enables various ES2015 Unicode features. You can use it to define a range of astral (non-BMP) symbols such as emojis, interpret surrogate pairs as whole characters, interpret Unicode property escapes, and more.

---

6.   https://mathiasbynens.be/notes/es6-unicode-regex

Recipe 44

Searching from a Specific Index with the y Flag

Task

Let's say your task is to take the transcript of a conference and organize it in a way that can be read like an article. Suppose the transcript is like this:

```
<p>2:05 pm: We also improved durability, which is another essential aspect
of our products.</p>

<p>2:10 pm: It has our most crack resistant front crystal, thanks to a
stronger and more robust geometry.</p>

<p>2:15 pm: It's also our first product to have IP6X certification, so you
don't have to worry about wearing it in dusty environments.</p>
```

And you want to remove the timestamps and extra <p></p> tags, and join the sentences like this:

```
<p>We also improved durability, which is another essential aspect of our
products. It has our most crack resistant front crystal, thanks to a stronger
and more robust geometry. It's also our first product to have IP6X
certification, so you don't have to worry about wearing it in dusty
environments.</p>
```

The data you want to extract has a fixed structure: a string in a pair of HTML tags and a timestamp that's always eight characters long. So, you just need to retrieve the characters from index 9 onwards.

Solution

Use the sticky flag (y) to match the target string only from the index you specify with the lastIndex property:

```
part_2/flag_sticky/sticky_ex1.js
const re = /.+/ys;

re.lastIndex = 9;

const str = `2:05 pm: We also improved durability, which is another essential
aspect of our products.`;

console.log(str.match(re)[0]);
// → We also improved durability, which is another essential aspect of our
// products.
```

Now that you know your regex works, use it to extract text from an actual HTML document:

part_2/flag_sticky/sticky.html

```html
<!doctype html>
<html lang="en-us">
<head>
  <meta charset="utf-8">
  <meta name="viewport" content="width=device-width, initial-scale=1">
  <script src="sticky_ex2.js" defer></script>
</head>
<body>
  <p>2:05 pm: We also improved durability, which is another essential aspect
  of our products.</p>
  <p>2:10 pm: It has our most crack resistant front crystal, thanks to a
  stronger and more robust geometry.</p>
  <p>2:15 pm: It's also our first product to have IP6X certification, so you
  don't have to worry about wearing it in dusty environments.</p>
</body>
</html>
```

Call the querySelectorAll() method to retrieve all paragraph elements, and pass each to a function that applies the regex, like this:

part_2/flag_sticky/sticky_ex2.js

```js
let result = "";

// Extract info from each element and append it to result
function extractData(str) {
  const re = /.+/ys;
  re.lastIndex = 9;
  const match = str.match(re);
  if (match) {
    result = result + match[0] + " ";
  } else {
    throw new Error("No match found.");
  }
}

// Execute extractData() for the content of each <p> element
document.querySelectorAll("p").forEach(el => {
  extractData(el.textContent);
});

// Remove newline characters from the resulting string,
// remove whitespace from both ends of the string,
// and enclose it in a pair of <p> tags.
console.log(`<p>${result.trim().replaceAll("\n", "")}</p>`);
```

You now have contiguous sentences that can be read like a story.

Discussion

The sticky flag performs a search only at the position indicated by the lastIndex property. Consider this code:

part_2/flag_sticky/sticky_ex3.js

```
Line 1  const str = "crack resistant";
   -    const re = /resistant/y;

   -    re.lastIndex = 0;
   5    console.log(str.match(re));
   -    // → null (no match at index 0)

   -    re.lastIndex = 2;
   -    console.log(str.match(re));
   10   // → null (no match at index 2)

   -    re.lastIndex = 6;
   -    console.log(str.match(re));
   -    // → ["resistant", index: 6, input: "crack resistant", groups: undefined]
   15
   -    console.log(re.lastIndex);
   -    // → 15
```

A sticky search won't match characters from any index other than the one indicated by the lastIndex property. Also, notice how the flag updates the lastIndex property when the operation is successful (Line 16).

The Order of Flags

JavaScript flags can be specified in any order or combination. The regex /abc/img behaves in the same way as /abc/mgi.

The sticky flag is useful when the string we want to match has a fixed structure. In this recipe, we knew ahead of time about the structure of the input string: a timestamp followed by a sentence. So we simplified the pattern by telling the engine to search only at the position where the data we want is located. Without the sticky flag, the pattern could become unnecessarily more complicated.

Recipe 45

Modifying an Existing Regex Literal

Task

Suppose you want to take your teammate's regular expression literal and modify it for use in another part of the code. You don't want to alter the original regex because it has passed all tests for the job it was intended for.

You need a solution that enables you to modify a copy of an existing regex literal.

Solution

Use the source and flags properties to retrieve the original regex parts. And construct a new RegExp object with those parts:

part_2/modifying_regex/modifying_regex_ex1.js
```
// Pattern to match a filename with .png extension
const origRegex = /\b(\w+)\.png\b/;

// Pattern to match a filename with .png or .PNG extension
const newRegex = new RegExp(origRegex.source, origRegex.flags + "i");
```

Hooray! You have successfully added the i flag to the regex pattern.

Discussion

JavaScript provides the flags property for reading all flags used in a regex:

part_2/modifying_regex/modifying_regex_ex2.js
```
const re1 = /\b(\w+)\.png\b/igu;
const re2 = /\b(\w+)\.png\b/;

console.log(re1.flags);    // → giu
console.log(re2.flags);    // → ""
```

Notice how the order of flags changes when reading them. The flags property always ignores the order of the original pattern and lists them in a fixed order: "gimuy." If the pattern has no flags, the return value will be an empty string.

Similarly, the source property gets us the pattern enclosed between the forward slashes:

```
part_2/modifying_regex/modifying_regex_ex3.js
const re = /\b(\w+)\.png\b/igu;

console.log(re.source);     // → \b(\w+)\.png\b
```

We can also check if a specific flag is applied to a regex. For example, to see if the global flag g is set, we can read the global property:

```
part_2/modifying_regex/modifying_regex_ex4.js
const re1 = /\b(\w+)\.png\b/ig;
const re2 = /\b(\w+)\.png\b/u;

console.log(re1.global);    // → true
console.log(re2.global);    // → false
```

The following table lists all supported flags along with their corresponding properties. Note that all these properties are read-only:

Flag	Corresponding Property
d	hasIndices
g	global
i	ignoreCase
m	multiline
s	dotAll
u	unicode
y	sticky

Use the flags property to retrieve the flags of a regex object. And use the source property to retrieve the source text of a regex object. Remember, the returned value by source is without the two forward slashes on the sides or flags. These properties are mainly helpful when you want to construct a new pattern from an existing one.

Recipe 46

Referencing a Matched String with the Backreference

Task

Suppose your task is to inspect documents for duplicate words, such as "the the book," which is a common typographical mistake with texts subject to heavy editing. The task involves looking for repeated words despite capitalization differences like "This this." It also requires finding instances with varying amounts of whitespace between the words, including tabs and newlines.

You need to come up with a solution that will find all duplicate words and automatically fix them.

Solution

Capture the word with a capturing group, and use a backreference to match the same text matched by the capturing group:

```
part_2/backreference/backreference_ex1.js
function dupWordRemover(str) {
  const re = /\b([-'\w]+)\s+\1\b/ig;
  return str.replace(re, "$1");
}

const str = "No no man has a  a good enough memory to be a successful liar.";

dupWordRemover(str)
// → "No man has a good enough memory to be a successful liar."
```

Problem solved! Your text is now free of most duplicate words.

The Importance of Evaluating Repeated Words Before Elimination

Keep in mind that the usage of repeated words is not always a mistake and eliminating them without evaluation can be risky. For instance, "had had" is the past perfect form of "have," and sometimes words like "ha ha" and other structures can produce intentionally repeated words. So, it makes sense to check out each match before getting rid of them.

Also note that this recipe only detects duplicated words consisting of ASCII word characters. If you want to include accented letters and letters from different writing systems, you should use the Unicode Letter category (see Recipe 53, Matching Unicode Word Boundaries with the Unicode Property Escape, on page 139).

Discussion

When there's a capturing group in a pattern, the content inside the parentheses is bookmarked. A backreference provides a convenient way to reuse this content in the form of \1, \2, and so forth, where \1 refers to the first captured group, \2 refers to the second captured group, and so on.

This approach is not the same as just repeating a token or group with a quantifier. To illustrate this, let's compare two simple regular expressions: \d{2} and (\d)\1. The first one uses a quantifier to match any two digits, while the second one uses a capturing group and backreference to match the same digit twice.

Now, let's take a look at the regex step by step:

```
/\b([-'\w]+)\s+\1\b/ig
```

- \b asserts the position at a word boundary
- ([-'\w]+) 1st capturing group
  - [-'\w] matches a single character present in the list below
    - - matches a - character literally
    - ' matches a ' character literally
    - \w matches any word character
  - + matches the previous token one or more times
- \s matches any whitespace character
  - + matches the previous token one or more times
- \1 matches the same text matched by the 1st capturing group
- \b asserts the position at a word boundary
- Flags
  - i: enables case-insensitive matching
  - g: enables global, which returns all matches

The regex in this recipe starts by matching a word boundary (\b). This ensures that we are only matching whole words. Then, we use a capturing group ([-'\w]+) to match one or more occurrences of any combination of letters, digits, underscores, hyphens, and apostrophes. It's important to match hyphens and apostrophes because we want to be able to detect repeated words such as "check-in check-in" and "can't can't."

After capturing the first word, we use \s+ to match one or more whitespace characters (such as spaces and tabs) between the first and second occurrence of the captured group. Next, we use the backreference \1 to ensure that the second occurrence is the same as the first. The regex ends with another word boundary (\b).

To execute the regex, we use the replace() method. replace() takes the regex as its first argument, attempts to find a match in the given string, and replaces it with its second argument. In this case, the replacement value is $1, which is a special replacement pattern for referring to the first capturing group. The result is that the matched substring, which is "No no," gets replaced with "No." For more on special replacement patterns, see Recipe 34, Using Special Replacement Patterns, on page 91.

We can use a backreference with a named capturing group, too—either with a regular numbered backreference or the \k<name> syntax. Let's look at an example:

```
part_2/backreference/backreference_ex2.js
function dupWordRemover(str) {
  const re = /\b(?<dup>[-'\w]+)\s+\k<dup>\b/ig;
  return str.replace(re, "$1");
}

const str = "No no man has a  a good enough memory to be a successful liar.";

dupWordRemover(str)
// → "No man has a good enough memory to be a successful liar."
```

This code achieves the same result as the solution in this recipe, except that it uses a named capturing group (?<dup>[-'\w]+) and references the group with \k<dup>. For more on named capturing groups, see Recipe 33, Reading Groups with Ease Using Named Capturing Groups, on page 89.

One difference between JavaScript's regular expression flavor and other flavors is the way it handles backreference. Unlike most flavors, JavaScript doesn't distinguish between a backreference to a capturing group that matched nothing, and a backreference to a capturing group that didn't participate in the match.

Let me clarify with a simple example: the regex /(-?)cat\1/ matches the string "cat," "-cat," or "-cat-." In JavaScript, this pattern is equivalent to /(-)?cat\1/. But that's different from most other regex flavors.

Here's how the regex engine in JavaScript processes /(-?)cat\1/ when applied to the string "cat." First, the regex engine attempts to match a hyphen (-) literally, and it successfully matches nothing (recall that ? is a metacharacter that matches zero or one occurrence of the preceding character).

The next character in the string is the letter c, and the engine successfully matches it. The engine also matches the next two characters: a and t. Finally, \1 successfully matches the same zero occurrences of - in the capturing group.

Now let's look at the second pattern: /(-)?cat\1/. Here, the engine cannot match -, but since there is a question mark after the capturing group, it becomes optional, and the engine proceeds to match the literal characters. The regex \1 refers to the capturing group that failed to match anything, resulting in a backreference that also fails to match.

There's no question mark after the backreference to make it optional, so the overall match fails in most flavors. But JavaScript is different. In JavaScript, a backreference to a capturing group that did not participate in the match successfully matches nothing, causing the overall match to succeed.

On one hand, it can be advantageous because you don't need to worry about whether a particular capturing group participated in the match or not. On the other hand, this lack of distinction can cause your pattern to fail in other regex flavors.

Reusing a Backreference

 A backreference can be reused more than once. For example, (ha)\1\1 matches hahaha.

Forward References

 JavaScript doesn't support forward references. A forward reference lets you reference a group that appears later in the regex.

Take advantage of a backreference to refer to the exact text matched by a capturing group. You can reuse the content in the form of \1, \2, and so on, when using a normal capturing group. If you are using a named capturing group, you can also use the \k<name> syntax.

Recipe 47

Testing a Pattern with the Positive Lookahead

Task

Suppose your task is to fix a mistake in several documents that inaccurately list a company's revenue in dollars, instead of euros. You need to find all instances of "$90.3 million" and replace "$" with "€."

So, what you need is a regex pattern that finds "$90.3 million" in a sentence such as this:

```
"The Company posted a September quarter record revenue of $90.3 million,
up 8 percent year over year."
```

But you want to match and replace only the currency sign, not the entire string. You need a way to exclude "90.3 million" from the match result.

Solution

Use a positive *lookahead* denoted by (?= ...) to match the part of the string that you don't want to include in the result:

```
part_2/positive_lookahead/positive_lookahead_ex1.js
const str = `The Company posted a September quarter record revenue
of $90.3 million, up 8 percent year over year.`;

const re = /\$(?=90\.3\smillion)/ig;

// Replace only $ with €
str.replace(re, "€");
// → "The Company posted a September quarter record revenue \n
// of €90.3 million, up 8 percent year over year."
```

With the (?= ...) syntax, you require a pattern to appear after the regex match without including it in the match.

Discussion

Lookaheads are non-capturing groups that allow us to match a pattern based on the substring that follows the pattern. For a positive lookahead match to be successful, it must match a pattern followed by the pattern in subexpression.

Notice the output of match() in the following code, which is only "$."

```
part_2/positive_lookahead/positive_lookahead_ex2.js
const str = "$90.3 million";
const re = /\$(?=90\.3\smillion)/;

str.match(re)[0];    // → "$"
```

When using a lookahead, the subexpression is not included in the result. It also can't be referenced with a backreference.

There's a workaround, though. If you place capturing parentheses around the expression in the lookahead like (?=(regex)), you can capture the match in lookarounds, too. Wrapping the entire lookahead in parentheses won't work because when the capturing group wants to store the match, the lookahead will already have discarded it.

Don't confuse capturing and matching. The positive lookahead assertion (?= ...) and the non-capturing group (?: ...) serve different purposes. While both don't capture the substring they match, the non-capturing group includes the substring in the overall match, while the positive lookahead assertion does not.

For example, if we rewrite the solution in this recipe to substitute a non-capturing group for the lookahead assertion, the entire match gets replaced:

part_2/positive_lookahead/positive_lookahead_ex3.js

```
const str = `The Company posted a September quarter record revenue
of $90.3 million, up 8 percent year over year.`;

const re = /\$(?:90\.3\smillion)/ig;

str.replace(re, "€");
// → "The Company posted a September quarter record revenue \n
// of €, up 8 percent year over year."
```

For more on non-capturing groups, see Recipe 31, Extracting a Matched Value with the Capturing Group, on page 86.

Now, let's dig a bit deeper into the regex pattern:

```
/\$(?=90\.3\smillion)/ig
```

- `\$` matches the character "$" literally
- `(?=90.3\smillion)` positive lookahead
  - `90` matches the characters "90" literally
  - `\.` matches the character "." literally
  - `3` matches the character "3" literally
  - `\s` matches any whitespace character
  - `million` matches the characters "million" literally
- Flags
- `i` case-insensitive match
- `g` global match

Use a lookahead to inspect whether it's possible to match a specific string without actually matching it. You have two types of lookaheads at your disposal: positive lookahead and negative lookahead. The positive lookahead is denoted by the (?= ...) syntax, and it ensures that a pattern is followed by another pattern. On the other hand, negative lookahead, which we will focus on in the next recipe, is denoted by (?! ...), and it guarantees that a pattern is not followed by another pattern.

Recipe 48

Testing a Pattern with the Negative Lookahead

Task

Suppose you want to match any two-digit number except 41, 66, and 77 because these are retired jersey numbers, so you want to make sure they don't get reassigned to a new player.

You could use several character classes matching a range between 00 to 40, 42 to 65, 67 to 76, and 78 to 99. But you'd end up with a very long and complicated pattern. Fortunately, there's a more compact way to get the same result with lookahead assertions.

Solution

Use a negative lookahead assertion denoted by (?! ...):

part_2/negative_lookahead/negative_lookahead_ex1.js
```
const re = /#(?!41|66|77)\d{2}/

re.test("#00");    // → true
re.test("#39");    // → true
re.test("#41");    // → false
re.test("#66");    // → false
re.test("#77");    // → false
re.test("#98");    // → true
```

A negative lookahead matches a pattern not followed by another pattern. In this code, the negative lookahead ensures that the string following "#" isn't "41," "66," or "77."

Discussion

Negative lookahead is a type of non-capturing group denoted by the syntax (?! ...), where the ... represents the pattern that should not be present immediately after the current position in the string.

Let's examine how the engine interprets the regex /#(?!(41|66|77))\d{2}/ when applied to the string "#39":

```
#39
|
# matches a hash sign literally.

#39
 |
(?!41|66|77) successfully matches a string that isn't 41, 66, or 77.
The pointer remains at #.

#39
 |
 \d matches a digit.

#39
  |
  \d matches a digit.
```

Lookaheads let you check whether you can match a specific string without actually matching it. Use a negative lookahead when you want to ensure a pattern does not follow another pattern.

Recipe 49

Testing a Pattern with the Positive Lookbehind

Task

Suppose your task is to extract questions from a standardized test and store them in a database. The info you're looking for always comes after a numbering system like "Question #5:", but you want to extract the question text without its numbering.

The sticky flag wouldn't be effective in this case because the length of characters in the numbering system varies between questions. For instance, one question may begin with "Question #9," while another question may start with "Question #10" (for more on the sticky flag, see Recipe 44, Searching from a Specific Index with the y Flag, on page 119).

You need a solution that allows you to match questions preceded by a "Question #n" without including the numbering in the result.

Solution

Enclose the pattern in a positive *lookbehind* assertion denoted by (?<= ...):

```
part_2/positive_lookbehind/positive_lookbehind_ex1.js
const re = /(?<=Question\s#\d{1,3}:\s).+?\./igs;
const str = `
Question #9: The Peloponnesian Wars were fought between _____.
Question #10: A ziggurat is _____.
`;

const questions = str.match(re);

console.log(questions);
// → [
//    "The Peloponnesian Wars were fought between _____.",
//    "A ziggurat is _____."
// ]
```

Success! The matched items don't include the numbering system.

Browser Compatibility

Although lookbehind assertions are supported by the latest version of modern browsers,[7] chances are not all of your users have updated their browsers. To ensure maximum compatibility, you can use lookbehind assertions on the server side, where they've been supported since Node 10.3.

Discussion

Before ES2018, JavaScript only supported *lookahead* assertions in regular expressions. But, with the introduction of ES2018, *lookbehinds* were added to enhance JavaScript capabilities. Similar to lookaheads, lookbehinds also come in two versions: positive and negative.

In this recipe, .+\. matches one or more characters until it reaches a full stop. But before that, there's a positive lookbehind that ensures the pattern is preceded by the word "Question" followed by a whitespace, a #, 1 to 3 digits, a :, and another whitespace.

Let's examine the regex pattern step by step:

```
/(?<=Question\s#\d{1,3}:\s).+\./igs
```

- `(?<=Question\s#\d:\s)` positive lookbehind
  - `Question` matches the characters "Question" literally
  - `\s` matches any whitespace character
  - `#` matches the character "#" literally
  - `\d` matches a digit
    - `{1,3}` matches the previous token between 1 and 3 times
  - `:` matches the character ":" literally
  - `\s` matches any whitespace character
- `.` matches any character
  - `+?` matches the previous token between one and unlimited times (lazy)
- `\.` matches the character "." literally
- Flags
  - `i` performs a case-insensitive match
  - `g` finds all matches
  - `s` dot matches newline characters

What's a Lookaround?

The lookahead and lookbehind assertions are collectively called *lookarounds*.

---

7.   https://caniuse.com/?search=lookbehind

Multiple Lookarounds

Several lookarounds of any sort (negative or positive) may appear in succession to create a more complex pattern.

The important thing to remember about lookarounds is that although they check if a match is possible, they don't actually consume the characters in the string. Lookbehinds are similar to lookaheads except that they work backward. They instruct the regex to briefly move backward in the string to see if their subexpression can match.

Recipe 50

Testing a Pattern with the Negative Lookbehind

Task

Suppose you're searching hospital records for a patient named Smith, but most of the data you get from search results is about Dr. Smith. You need a regex that matches "Smith" but excludes "Dr. Smith."

Solution

Use a negative lookbehind assertion denoted by (?<! ...):

```
part_2/negative_lookbehind/negative_lookbehind_ex1.js
const re = /(?<!Dr\.\s)Smith/;

console.log(re.test("Dr. Smith"));     // → false
console.log(re.test("Mr. Smith"));     // → true
console.log(re.test("John Smith"));    // → true
```

Your regex now finds all records containing "Smith" except for "Dr. Smith."

Discussion

The negative version of lookbehind asserts that the pattern within the lookbehind does not precede a pattern. In this case, we're using it to ensure that the word "Smith" isn't preceded by an uppercase D, a lowercase r, a period (.), and a whitespace character (\s). You must use a backslash to escape the period; otherwise, the regex engine will interpret it as a metacharacter.

Not Just at the Beginning

Lookbehinds can be used anywhere in the regex, not just at the beginning.

Table of Groups

In addition to lookarounds, regular expressions provide several types of groups that are constructed using a pair of parentheses, with the opening parenthesis immediately followed by a question mark. For easier comparison, we've summarized the syntax for these groups in the following table. Keep this table bookmarked—it's sure to come in handy:

Metacharacter	Meaning
(...)	Capturing group
(?: ...)	Non-capturing group
(?= ...)	Positive lookahead
(?! ...)	Negative lookahead
(?<= ...)	Positive lookbehind
(?<! ...)	Negative lookbehind

The takeaway from this recipe is to use a negative lookbehind when you want to match a pattern not preceded by a specific pattern.

Recipe 51

Matching Non-ASCII Numerals with the Unicode Property Escape

Task

Let's say you want to match a number in a language that has a different numeral system, such as Persian or Vietnamese. Remember Recipe 29, Repeating Part of a Regex with Quantifiers, on page 80, where you validated a PIN code with regex?

This time you want to allow users to use numerals in their own language to create a PIN. But, the problem is that the character class for matching digits (\d) matches only ASCII digits:

part_2/unicode_property_escapes_p1/upe_p1_ex1.js

```
const re = /^\d{4,6}$/;

// digits in the Persian language
// equivalent to 1234
const str = "۱۲۳۴";

re.test(str);
// → false
```

Even setting the Unicode flag won't help:

part_2/unicode_property_escapes_p1/upe_p1_ex2.js

```
const re = /^\d{4,6}$/u;

// digits in the Persian language
const str = "۱۲۳۴";

re.test(str);
// → false
```

You need a solution that lets you verify digits in any language.

Solution

Use a Unicode property escape in the form of \p{Number}:

part_2/unicode_property_escapes_p1/upe_p1_ex3.js

```
const re = /^\p{Number}{4,6}$/u;

// digits in Persian
re.test("۱۲۳۴");        // → true

// digits in Thai
re.test("๑๒๓๔");        // → true

// digits in Tamil
re.test("௫௨௬௭");        // → true
```

Success! You've matched digits in three different languages.

Discussion

Symbols in the Unicode standard have various properties and property values. With Unicode property escapes, regex can match characters based on their Unicode properties.

In this recipe, we're using \p{Number} to match every symbol in the Number category, including Roman numerals and numbers classified as compatibly equivalent:

part_2/unicode_property_escapes_p1/upe_p1_ex4.js

```
const re = /^\p{Number}{4,6}$/u;

console.log(re.test("VIXIVVIII"));   // → true
console.log(re.test("①②③④"));        // → true
```

If you want to exclude non-decimal numbers, you can use \p{Decimal_Number} instead:

part_2/unicode_property_escapes_p1/upe_p1_ex5.js

```
const re = /\p{Decimal_Number}/u;

console.log(re.test("VIXIVVIII"));    // → false
console.log(re.test("½¼¾½"));         // → false
console.log(re.test("١٢٣٤"));         // → true
```

Remember, it's possible to use Unicode property escapes only when the u flag is set. If no u flag is present, then the pattern \p is a redundant escape sequence for the letter p. This is by design so that existing patterns that might use \p{ ... } wouldn't break with the introduction of the Unicode property escapes into the language.

Negated Unicode Property Escapes

 Unicode property escapes also have a negated version denoted by \P{ ... }, which lets you match the opposite of what they normally match. For example, if you wanted to match a string that doesn't have a number, you'd write:

```
/^\P{Number}+$/u
```

In this recipe, we used \p{Number} to match symbols in the Number category, but you can also match other types of symbols. The next recipe shows you how to take advantage of *Unicode property escapes* to match a word character.

Recipe 52

Matching Non-ASCII Words with the Unicode Property Escape

Task

Let's assume you want to search for a file with a specific extension and extract the filename. This task is similar to Recipe 31, Extracting a Matched Value with the Capturing Group, on page 86, where you matched a file with a .pdf extension.

Now you want to match a filename that has non-ASCII characters. It's not uncommon for people to save files in their own language, but your current script is unable to match non-ASCII letters:

```
part_2/unicode_property_escapes_p2/upe_p2_ex1.js
const re = /\b(\w+)\.pdf\b/;

const str = "Please click on شاهنامه.pdf to download the file.";
const result = str.match(re);

if (result) {
  console.log(result[1])
} else {
  console.error("No match found.");
}
// logs:
// → No match found.
```

You need a solution that allows you to match non-ASCII words.

Solution

Use a combination of Unicode property escapes to match Unicode word characters in the same way \w matches ASCII word characters:

```
part_2/unicode_property_escapes_p2/upe_p2_ex2.js
const re = /([\p{Alpha}\p{Pc}\p{Mark}\p{Nd}\p{Join_Control}]+)\.pdf\b/u;

const str = "Please click on شاهنامه.pdf to download the file.";
const result = str.match(re);

if (result) {
  console.log(result[1])
} else {
  console.error("No match found.");
}

// logs:
// → شاهنامه
```

Now you can match a filename in any language!

Discussion

The \w character class matches any alphanumeric character from the basic Latin alphabet, including the underscore. To match a similar range of characters but in Unicode, we need to use multiple property escapes:

- \p{Alpha} is short for Alphabetic and matches any character with the Alphabetic property

- \p{Pc} is an abbreviation for Connector_Punctuation, which matches a connecting punctuation mark, like an underscore

- \p{Mark} matches a combining mark

- \p{Nd} is an abbreviation for Decimal_Number and matches a decimal digit

- \p{Join_Control} matches format control characters that have functions for control of cursive joining and ligation

In the Unicode Standard, each character is assigned a set of properties and property values. The Unicode property escape enables us to match a character based on a particular property. For example, the letter "A" has an Alphabetic property with a value of Yes, which means we can match it with \p{Alpha} or \p{Alphabetic}.

To see the properties of a particular character, visit the Unicode character database and enter the character in the search bar.[8] For a list of supported property escapes, refer to the Unicode specification.[9]

---

8. https://util.unicode.org/UnicodeJsps/character.jsp?a=A&B1=Show
9. https://unicode.org/reports/tr18/

Recipe 53

Matching Unicode Word Boundaries with the Unicode Property Escape

Task

Suppose you want to search a document for the Portuguese word "vã," which means "go," without matching other words that contain "vã," such as "vão." To achieve this, you try using word boundaries to isolate the word "vã" from other words containing similar characters:

```
part_2/unicode_property_escapes_p3/upe_p3_ex1.js
const re = /\bvã\b/;

"vão".match(re);
// → ["vã", index: 0, input: "vão bem", groups: undefined]

"vã bem".match(re);
// → null
```

But, your regex is matching the opposite of your intended result. The problem is that the word boundary (\b) considers accented characters such as "ã" as non-word characters. You need an alternative solution that doesn't share the same limitation.

Solution

Use a combination of Unicode property escapes to match word boundaries in Unicode characters:

```
part_2/unicode_property_escapes_p3/upe_p3_ex2.js
let re = /(?<=[^\p{L}\p{M}\p{Nd}\p{Pc}]|^)vã(?=[^\p{L}\p{M}\p{Nd}\p{Pc}]|$)/u;

"vão".match(re);
// → null

"vã bem".match(re);
// → ["vã", index: 0, input: 'vã bem', groups: undefined]
```

Successful outcome! The regex is now able to correctly match the word boundary in Portuguese and other languages.

Discussion

When dealing with non-English text in JavaScript, one drawback is that the word boundary in the regex engine identifies only characters present in the ASCII table. As a result, \b fails to match a "complete word" when performing a search in text containing accented characters or words written in non-Latin scripts.

In this recipe, the issue arises because the character "ã" is classified as a non-word character, resulting in the detection of a word boundary between the letters "ã" and "o." Conversely, "ã" followed by a space character creates a continuous string of non-word characters, and therefore, no word boundary is detected.

To resolve this problem, we can use a set of Unicode property escapes in a lookaround:

- \p{L} Letter category: matches any type of letter regardless of the language

- \p{M} Mark category: matches a combining character, which is meant to be joined with another character such as accents, umlauts, enclosing boxes, and so on

- \p{Nd} Decimal digit number: matches any digit between 0 and 9 in any script, excluding ideographic scripts

- \p{Pc} Connector punctuation: matches a punctuation character, such as an underscore

Dealing with non-English text in JavaScript requires special attention to ensure accurate searching and matching of words. Using the standard word boundary can lead to incomplete matches for accented or non-Latin script words. Fortunately, by using Unicode property escapes, we can address this issue and achieve more reliable searches for non-English text.

Wrapping Up

Text processing is an essential part of any modern application. Whether you're working on a content-heavy website or building a sophisticated data analysis tool, using regular expressions can significantly enhance your development capabilities.

In this part of the book, you discovered how to use regex in JavaScript and take advantage of various regex methods. You learned about the building blocks of regex, such as character classes, quantifiers, and metacharacters, and how to combine them to form more complex patterns.

Up next, you'll bolster your understanding of regex by solving a wide range of text manipulation problems that require using the tokens discussed in this part. Regex may seem daunting at first, but with practice and patience, mastering this tool can significantly enhance your text-processing capabilities.

CHAPTER 3

Part III: Mastering Text Processing in JavaScript

Welcome to the final part of the book! In this part, get ready to tackle some engaging text-processing challenges. You'll have the opportunity to apply the syntax and techniques you've learned in the previous sections to handle a wide range of retrieval and alteration tasks. For example, you'll:

- Extract specific information from large datasets
- Clean and format data for easier analysis
- Automate repetitive tasks that would otherwise be time-consuming

Working through these recipes will strengthen your problem-solving abilities in the JavaScript language. As you become more proficient, you'll be able to apply your newfound knowledge in more effective ways. Solving thorny text-processing challenges will become second nature, and you'll be able to breeze through such tasks. So let's get started!

Recipe 54

Validating Email Addresses

Task

Suppose you have a form on your website or app that asks the user for an email address. Whether it's for sending newsletters, regular communication, password recovery, or any other purpose, ensuring that you have the correct email address is crucial before proceeding—to minimize the number of emails returned as undeliverable.

What you need is a mechanism to check that the entered text conforms to a valid email address format.

Solution

If your form is on a website, you can start by setting up the built-in HTML5 form features. First, ensure that your input element has a type attribute with a value of "email":

part_3/validating_email/email_ex1.html

```html
<form>
  <label for="Email">Email:</label>
  <input type="email" id="Email">
  <input type="submit">
</form>
```

Email inputs usually catch the most obvious errors that the user makes when typing their email. To enforce mandatory input, the easiest validation tool is the required attribute. To implement it, include the attribute right before the closing input tag:

part_3/validating_email/email_ex2.html

```html
<form>
  <label for="Email">Email:</label>
  <input type="email" id="Email" required>
  <input type="submit">
</form>
```

On the server-side, verify that the input has an at sign (@) that's preceded and followed by non-whitespace characters:

part_3/validating_email/email_ex2.js

```js
function isValidEmail(str) {
  const re = /^\S+@\S+$/;
  return re.test(str);
}

isValidEmail("faraz@");                 // → false
isValidEmail("@abcd");                  // → false
isValidEmail("faraz@somewhere.com");    // → true
```

This pattern performs a check similar to the HTML mechanism for validating emails.

Discussion

Designing web forms has always been challenging for programmers. Although coding the form itself is straightforward, verifying that every input has a logical and acceptable value poses a greater difficulty, and communicating any issues to the user can be a headache. Client-side form validation helps users identify and correct errors in their form submissions more quickly.

But, it's important to understand that relying solely on client-side validation may not provide comprehensive security. To ensure maximum security, your applications must perform security checks on form data on both the server-side and client-side. And regex is often the preferred tool for programmers to perform that task.

In most cases, the regex patterns you come across on the internet are excessively limiting for email address verification. Some developers recommend checking the input to conform to the RFC 5322 standard. RFC 5322 defines the structure and syntax of email messages, which includes the email addresses.[1]

To do that, you'll need a regex like this:

```
const re = /(?:[a-z0-9!#$%&'*+/=?^_`{|}~-]+(?:\.[a-z0-9!#$%&'*+/=?^_`{|}~-]+
)*|"(?:[\x01-\x08\x0b\x0c\x0e-\x1f\x21\x23-\x5b\x5d-\x7f]|\\[\x01-\x09\x0b\x
0c\x0e-\x7f])*")@(?:(?:[a-z0-9](?:[a-z0-9-]*[a-z0-9])?\.)+[a-z0-9](?:[a-z0-9
-]*[a-z0-9])?|\[(?:(?:(2(5[0-5]|[0-4][0-9])|1[0-9][0-9]|[1-9]?[0-9]))\.){3}(
?:(2(5[0-5]|[0-4][0-9])|1[0-9][0-9]|[1-9]?[0-9])|[a-z0-9-]*[a-z0-9]:(?:[\x01
-\x08\x0b\x0c\x0e-\x1f\x21-\x5a\x53-\x7f]|\\[\x01-\x09\x0b\x0c\x0e-\x7f])+)\
])/;
```

This regex is equally intimidating to developers who are unfamiliar with regular expressions and those who are proficient in them! But even validating an email address according to the RFC standard doesn't provide any information about the existence of the address at the given domain or the true ownership of the address.

According to RFC 5322, qwerty@qwerty.qwerty is a valid email address. However, it's not considered valid if the definition of a valid email address specifies that it must accept email. This is because there is no top-level domain called *qwerty*.[2]

---

1.   https://www.rfc-editor.org/rfc/rfc5322
2.   https://en.wikipedia.org/wiki/List_of_Internet_top-level_domains

Previously, it was logical to restrict the top-level domain to two-letter pairings for country codes and to perform a complete enumeration of generic top-level domains, like com|net|org|mil|edu. But as new top-level domains are added frequently, such patterns that were once valid quickly become outdated.

Basically, you can't be sure if david@somewhere.com can actually get emails unless you send one and see if it goes through. Even in this scenario, it's uncertain whether the absence of a reply indicates that the domain somewhere.com is discreetly getting rid of emails sent to non-existent mail addresses, or if David himself deleted them, or if his spam filter intercepted them.

A reliable email validation tool will do more than just check the syntax of the email address or ping a mail server. This process involves sending a message to the email address entered, which includes a confirmation token. Confirmation tokens are the only way to verify that the email address entered is correct.

That's why the majority of mailing lists rely on this mechanism to authenticate sign-ups. Because anyone can enter ceo@microsoft.com, which could be technically valid, yet it's improbable that the person at the receiving end is the actual CEO.

Because you need to send a confirmation email to verify whether an address exists or not, you have the option to choose a less strict regular expression. It may be better to let some invalid addresses pass through than to inconvenience people by blocking valid ones. Even though the solution in this recipe allows characters like %#$ that aren't typically found in email addresses, it's efficient and uncomplicated. Additionally, it will not prevent a legitimate email address from being accepted.

If you want to add complexity to your regex, my suggestion would be to notify the user that there could be an issue with the email address rather than making it forbidden.

> Recipe 55

Validating Password Strength

Task

Suppose your task is to check whether the passwords entered by users when signing up for a user account on your website are resistant to guessing or brute-force attacks. Usually, companies establish a password policy that outlines the criteria for creating and using passwords, which set requirements such as:

- Having a minimum length of 8 characters or more
- Containing both uppercase and lowercase letters
- Containing one or more numerical digits
- Containing special characters like @, #, $, etc
- Forbidding words listed in the password blocklist
- Forbidding words related to the user's personal information
- Forbidding the use of the company name or its abbreviation
- Forbidding passwords that match the date of birth, license plate number, phone number, or other frequently used numbers

The specific guidelines for usage can vary significantly depending on the business and system. So, this recipe provides a variety of regexes that you can use as building blocks to create customized validation rules according to your needs.

For matching non-English characters/digits, use the Unicode variants represented by \p{...} along with the u flag.

Solution

Containing at least one ASCII uppercase letter (recall that (?= ...) is a positive lookahead):

```
(?=.*[A-Z])
```

Containing at least one Unicode uppercase letter:

```
(?=.*\p{Uppercase})
```

\p{...} Requires a Flag

Don't forget to use the u flag when matching Unicode characters.

Containing at least one ASCII lowercase letter:

`(?=.*[a-z])`

Containing at least one Unicode lowercase letter:

`(?=.*\p{Lowercase})`

Containing at least one Unicode alphabet:

`(?=.*\p{Alphabetic})`

Containing at least one digit:

`(?=.*\d)`

Containing at least one Unicode digit:

`(?=.*\p{Number})`

Containing ASCII printable characters only:

`(?=.*[ -~])`

What Are ASCII Printable Characters?

ASCII printable characters consist of 95 characters that you can find on your QWERTY keyboard.[3] `(?=.*[ -~])` would match all ASCII printable characters from the space to the tilde, excluding the Delete character.

Containing one or more ASCII punctuations or spaces:

`(?=.*[ !"#$%&'()*+,\-./:;<=>?@[\\\]^_`{|}~])`

Containing anything other than ASCII letters and numbers:

`(?=.*[^A-Za-z0-9])`

Requiring a length of at least 8 characters:

`(?=.{8,})`

---

3.   https://www.ascii-code.com/

Requiring a length of at least 8 characters and a maximum of 32 characters:

```
(?=.{8,32})
```

Containing two or more digits/letters:

```
(?=(.*[a-z]){2,})     // at least 2 lowercase ASCII letters
(?=(.*[A-Z]){2,})     // at least 2 uppercase ASCII letters
(?=(.*[0-9]){2,})     // at least 2 ASCII digits
```

You can also use this technique to require multiple punctuations, Unicode characters, and so on.

Example: minimum eight characters, one ASCII letter, and one special character:

part_3/validating_passwords/pass_ex1.js
```
let re = /^(?=.*[A-Za-z])(?=.*[ !"#$%&'()*+,\-./:;<=>?@[\\\]^_`{|}~]).{8,}$/;

re.test("abcdefgh");      // → false
re.test("A7#cdefgh");     // → true
```

Example: minimum eight characters, two Unicode digits, and two Unicode alphabets:

part_3/validating_passwords/pass_ex2.js
```
let re = /^(?=(.*\p{Alphabetic}){2,})(?=(.*\p{Number}){2,}).{8,}$/u;

re.test("a7bcdefgh");     // → false
re.test("a77bcdefg");     // → true
```

Example: forbidding words listed in a password blocklist:

While you can use regex to accomplish this task, JavaScript already offers a built-in method that streamlines the process:

part_3/validating_passwords/pass_ex3.js
```
let blocklist = ["asdasd", "qwerty", "password", "abc123", "qwerty123",
"iloveyou", "football", "princess", "superman", "computer"];

let pass = "superman";

blocklist.includes(pass);     // → true
```

Allowing Multiline Passwords

To ensure that your regex works correctly for complicated passwords containing line breaks, use the s flag (see Recipe 42, Forcing . to Match Newline Characters with the s Flag, on page 113).

Discussion

Users tend to select uncomplicated or commonly used passwords that are easy to recall. Surprisingly, some people are still using "123456" and "password" as their password, which means they are easy to hack. As a result, it's often necessary to safeguard users from choosing easy-to-guess passwords by implementing minimum password complexity requirements.

We structured each validation rule of this recipe into its own lookahead group. Without lookahead, you'd need to use multiple regex patterns or iterate over the string multiple times to check for all the required conditions, which can be less efficient and harder to maintain.

Lookaheads allow you to check for the conditions without actually advancing the position of the regex engine in the string, so each test runs from the start of the string. Once a lookahead succeeds, the regex engine then moves on to test the next lookahead from the same position. If a lookahead fails to find a match, the entire match fails as a result.

To search for a pattern, each lookahead has a ".*", which means that the character type being sought can appear anywhere in the string, not just at the beginning. With the technique illustrated here, you can include multiple password tests in a single regex.

Remember, it's important to validate form input with both client-side and server-side scripts. Client-side validation can provide immediate feedback to the user and can prevent errors from being submitted to the server. But, this type of validation can be bypassed or manipulated by users, either intentionally or unintentionally, and so cannot be relied upon as the only form of validation.

Recipe 56

Validating Social Security Numbers

Task

Suppose you have a loan application form (or maybe a background check form) and want to perform a check to ensure that the Social Security number (SSN) provided by users conforms to the standard format of an SSN.

The SSN is a nine-digit number that is divided into three parts separated by hyphens: AAA-GG-SSSS. The first set of three digits is called the area number, as it was once assigned based on geographical region. But it cannot be 000, 666, or between 900 and 999.

The group number, which consists of digits four and five, ranges from 01 to 99. The last four digits are known as serial numbers and are assigned from 0001 to 9999. You need a solution that adheres to all these rules and lets you quickly identify invalid SSNs.

Solution

Use the following function:

```
part_3/validating_ssn/ssn_ex1.js
function isValidSSN(ssn) {
  const re = /^(?!666|000)[0-8]\d{2}-(?!00)\d{2}-(?!0000)\d{4}$/;
  return re.test(ssn);
}

isValidSSN("123-45-6789");    // → true
isValidSSN("123-456-789");    // → false
isValidSSN("123-00-6789");    // → false
isValidSSN("666-45-6789");    // → false
```

This function ensures that the format of the SSN is correct and that it contains the correct number of digits, thus minimizing data entry errors.

Discussion

The regex in this recipe matches a valid SSN that has the format XXX-XX-XXXX, where the first three digits are not 666 or 000, the fourth and fifth digits are not 00, and the last four digits are not 0000.

(?!000|666) at the beginning of the pattern is a negative lookahead assertion that prevents matching SSNs that start with 666 or 000, which are invalid SSNs. The pattern matches any two- or four-digit number in its second and third sets of digits. But, it incorporates a negative lookahead beforehand to avoid matching zeros.

Here is the regex pattern with explanations for each segment:

```
/^(?!666|000)[0-8]\d{2}-(?!00)\d{2}-(?!0000)\d{4}$/
```

- `^` asserts the position at start of the string
- `(?!666|000)` negative lookahead: assert that the regex below does not match.
  - 1st Alternative
    - 666 matches the characters 666 literally

○ 2nd Alternative
   ○ 000 matches the characters 000 literally
● [0-8] matches a single character in the range between 0 and 8
● \d matches a digit
  ○ {2} matches the previous token exactly 2 times
● - matches a hyphen character
● (?!00) negative lookahead: asserts that the regex doesn't match 00
● \d matches a digit
  ○ {2} matches the previous token exactly 2 times
● - matches a hyphen character
● (?!0000) negative lookahead: asserts that the regex doesn't match 0000
● \d matches a digit
  ○ {4} matches the previous token exactly 4 times
● $ asserts the position at the end of the string

After confirming that the provided value adheres to the standard format of the Social Security number, you might consider employing a more strict approach, which involves verifying with the Social Security Administration that the number corresponds to an existing individual.[4]

Keep in mind the significance of validating Social Security numbers to avoid administrative errors during the processing of important documents such as official records.

Recipe 57

Validating ZIP Codes

Task

Suppose you run an online shop that is dedicated to delivering packages to customers as quickly as possible. So, you want to ensure the ZIP codes (postal codes used in the United States) entered by users conform to a standard format to prevent errors in mail delivery. The basic format of a ZIP code consists of five digits. But, there's an extended ZIP+4 code which features the five digits of the ZIP code, followed by a hyphen and four digits that define a more precise location.

---

4.   https://www.ssa.gov/employer/ssnv.htm

You aim to create a regular expression capable of matching input formats such as 12345, 12345-6789, and 12345 6789, while excluding 1234, 123456, 123456789, or 1234-56789.

Solution

Use the following function:

part_3/validating_zipcode/zipcode_ex1.js
```
function isValidZipCode(zipcode) {
  const re = /^\d{5}(?:[-\s]\d{4})?$/;
  return re.test(zipcode);
}

isValidZipCode("12345-6789");    // → true
isValidZipCode("12345 6789");    // → true
isValidZipCode("12345");         // → true
isValidZipCode("123456789");     // → false
isValidZipCode("1234-56789");    // → false
isValidZipCode("123456");        // → false
isValidZipCode("1234");          // → false
```

With this code, you can verify that a given ZIP code conforms to the standard format used by the United States Postal Service (USPS).

Discussion

The function in this recipe takes a ZIP code as input and returns true if it's a valid US ZIP code (5 digits or 5 digits followed by a space/hyphen and 4 digits) and false otherwise. A detailed explanation of the regex is as follows:

/^\d{5}(?:[-\s]\d{4})?$/

- ^ asserts the position at start of the string
- \d matches a digit
  - {5} matches the previous token exactly 5 times
- (?:[-\s]\d{4}) non-capturing group
  - [-\s] matches a single character in the list
    - - matches the character - literally
    - \s matches any whitespace character
  - \d matches a digit
    - {4} matches the previous token exactly 4 times
- ? matches the previous token 0 or 1 time
- $ asserts the position at the end of the string

This regex assumes that the provided string consists solely of a ZIP code. But, if you intend to locate ZIP codes within a larger document or input string, you should substitute ^ and $ with the word boundary like this: /\b\d{5}(?:[-\s]\d{4})?\b/.

Checking the validity of ZIP codes in forms is crucial because it helps to avoid errors in address data, ensuring that goods or services are delivered to the correct recipient and preventing unnecessary delays or expenses.

Recipe 58

Validating Canadian Postal Codes

Task

Let's suppose you have a specialized shop catering to your Canadian customers, and you want to ensure that the postal code entered by users is a valid Canadian postal code.

In Canada, a postal code is a combination of six characters that includes both letters and digits. The format of the code follows A1A 1A1, where the letter A represents any letter of the alphabet and the number 1 represents any digit. The third and fourth characters are separated by a single space.

For example, the postal code for the CN Tower in Toronto is M5V 1J2. You want to create a regex matching the format of that postal code, but not invalid patterns like A1A 1A1A, 111 111, A1A1A1, A1A-A1A, or 12A 1B1.

Solution

Use the following function:

```
part_3/validating_ca_postal/ca_postal_ex1.js
function isValidPostalCode(postalCode) {
  const re = /^(?!.*[DFIOQU])[A-VXY][0-9][A-Z]\s[0-9][A-Z][0-9]$/;
  return re.test(postalCode);
}

isValidPostalCode("A1A 1A1A");    // → false
isValidPostalCode("111 111");     // → false
isValidPostalCode("A1A1A1");      // → false
isValidPostalCode("A1A-A1A");     // → false
isValidPostalCode("12A 1B1");     // → false
isValidPostalCode("M5V 1J2");     // → true
```

This code enables you to confirm whether a provided input conforms to the Canadian postal code format.

Discussion

The regex in this recipe begins with a negative lookahead that prohibits the occurrence of D, F, I, O, Q, or U at any position within the string. Because of their resemblance to other characters, the letters D, F, I, O, Q, and U are excluded from Canadian postal codes. This is because D, I, and O can be confused with 0, 1, and 0 respectively, while F, Q, and U can be mistaken for E, 0, and V.

The pattern .* at the beginning of the negative lookahead tells the regex engine that the character type being sought can appear anywhere in the string, not just at the beginning.

Canadian postal codes cannot start with the letters W or Z. To ensure that the first character of the string is not W or Z, we use the character class [A-VXY]. This tells the regex engine that the character must be any letter from A to V or X or Y, but not W or Z.

With the exception of the two aforementioned cases, Canadian postal codes follow a straightforward pattern of six alternating alphanumeric characters, with the option of a single space in the middle.

Let's dig a bit deeper into the pattern:

```
/^(?!.*[DFIOQU])[A-VXY][0-9][A-Z]\s[0-9][A-Z][0-9]$/
```

- ^ asserts the position at start of the string
- (?!.*[DFIOQU]) negative lookahead: asserts the regex below doesn't match
  - . matches any character (except for line terminators)
  - * matches the previous token between zero and unlimited times, as many times as possible
  - [DFIOQU] matches a single character in the list DFIOQU
- [A-VXY] matches a single character present in the list below
  - A-V matches a single character in the range between A and V
  - XY matches a single character in the list XY
- [0-9] matches a single character in the range between 0 and 9
- [A-Z] matches a single character in the range between A and Z
- \s matches any whitespace character
- [0-9] matches a single character in the range between 0 and 9
- [A-Z] matches a single character in the range between A and Z
- [0-9] matches a single character in the range between 0 and 9
- $ asserts the position at the end of the string

To locate a Canadian postal code in a string, substitute ^ and $ with word boundaries (\b): /\b(?!.*[DFIOQU])[A-VXY][0-9][A-Z]\s[0-9][A-Z][0-9]\b/.

By validating postal codes, you can avoid errors in address data, resulting in more efficient and reliable delivery of goods or services to the intended recipient.

Removing Duplicate Lines

Task

Suppose you need to display team rankings on a website, but your data was imported from another source and there were errors during the import process. So now, your new document has consecutive duplicate lines.

For instance, let's say your imported data consists of the lines below:

```
Team Power Rankings
#1  Cleveland Cavaliers 45-28
#2  Philadelphia 76ers 48-22
#2  Philadelphia 76ers 48-22
#3  Memphis Grizzlies 43-27
#4  Boston Celtics 49-23
#4  Boston Celtics 49-23
#4  Boston Celtics 49-23
```

Before you display the rankings, you need to remove the duplicates so that it gets displayed like this:

```
Team Power Rankings
#1  Cleveland Cavaliers 45-28
#2  Philadelphia 76ers 48-22
#3  Memphis Grizzlies 43-27
#4  Boston Celtics 49-23
```

You need a regex that can detect two identical lines and remove one of them.

Solution

Use the following function:

```
part_3/removing_dup_lines_v1/dup_lines_v1_ex1.js
function removeDuplicateLines(str) {
  const re = /^(.*)(?:\r?\n\1)+$/mg;
  return str.replace(re, "$1");
}

const str =
`Team Power Rankings
#1  Cleveland Cavaliers 45-28
#2  Philadelphia 76ers 48-22
#2  Philadelphia 76ers 48-22
```

```
#3  Memphis Grizzlies 43-27
#4  Boston Celtics 49-23
#4  Boston Celtics 49-23
#4  Boston Celtics 49-23`;

const result = removeDuplicateLines(str);

console.log(result);
// Team Power Rankings
// #1  Cleveland Cavaliers 45-28
// #2  Philadelphia 76ers 48-22
// #3  Memphis Grizzlies 43-27
// #4  Boston Celtics 49-23
```

This will output the string with any duplicate lines removed.

Discussion

To match the beginning of a line using regex, we use the symbol ^ at the start. Typically, ^ only matches the start of the string, so it's important to enable the multiline flag (m) to ensure that ^ and $ match at line breaks. Also make sure you don't use the dotAll flag (s) that allows the dot to match line breaks because that would lead to the regex matching the whole string.

We use a pair of parentheses containing .* to match the complete content of a line, including empty lines. Since the parentheses are a capturing group, we can later refer to the matched value with a backreference.

Within a non-capturing group (?: ...), we have used the pattern \r?\n\1 to identify line separators found in Unix and Unix-like systems (\n) or Windows/DOS (\r\n) text files. Next, we attempt to match the line that was previously matched with the backreference \1.

If the line at that position does not match, the matching process fails and the regex engine proceeds to the next match attempt. Conversely, if a match is found, we use the + quantifier to repeat the group, which consists of a line break and backreference, to match any subsequent identical lines.

Below is the breakdown of the regex pattern:

```
/^(.*)(?:\r?\n\1)+$/mg;
```

- `^` asserts the start of a line
- `(.*)` 1st capturing group
  - `.` matches any character except for line terminators
  - `*` matches the previous token zero or more times
- `(?:\r?\n\1)` non-capturing group
  - `\r` matches a carriage return
  - `?` matches the previous token zero or one time

- ○ \n matches a line-feed (newline) character
- ○ \1 matches the same text matched by the 1st capturing group
- • + matches the previous token one or more times
- • $ asserts the end of a line
- • Flags
  - ○ m: enables multiline, allowing ^ and $ to match line start and end
  - ○ g: enables global matching, which returns all matches

Because we are performing a search and replace operation, the complete match, which includes the original line and any line breaks, is eliminated from the string. To restore the initial line, we use the special replacement pattern $1 in the second argument of replace().

Removing duplicate lines with this technique is fast, but it won't remove duplicate lines that are separated by other lines. The next recipe shows you how to do that with JavaScript's built-in methods.

Recipe 60

Removing Duplicate Lines Separated by Other Lines

Task

Suppose you want to eliminate duplicated lines that are not adjacent to each other like in the previous recipe. For instance, let's say you have text like this:

```
Team Power Rankings
#1  Cleveland Cavaliers 45-28
#2  Philadelphia 76ers 48-22
#1  Cleveland Cavaliers 45-28
#3  Memphis Grizzlies 43-27
#2  Philadelphia 76ers 48-22
#4  Boston Celtics 49-23
```

And you need to write a code that outputs:

```
Team Power Rankings
#1  Cleveland Cavaliers 45-28
#2  Philadelphia 76ers 48-22
#3  Memphis Grizzlies 43-27
#4  Boston Celtics 49-23
```

Your code should have the capability to remove duplicate entries, even if they are interspersed with other lines.

Solution

Convert the string to an array, then pass the array to the Set constructor to remove duplicates, and finally convert the resulting Set to a string:

part_3/removing_dup_lines_v2/removing_dup_lines_v2_ex1.js
```
function removeDuplicateLines(str) {
  const arr = str.split(/\r?\n/);
  const set = [...new Set(arr)];
  const newStr = set.join("\n");
  return newStr;
}

const str =
`Team Power Rankings
#1  Cleveland Cavaliers 45-28
#2  Philadelphia 76ers 48-22
#1  Cleveland Cavaliers 45-28
#3  Memphis Grizzlies 43-27
#2  Philadelphia 76ers 48-22
#4  Boston Celtics 49-23`;

const result = removeDuplicateLines(str);

console.log(result);
// Team Power Rankings
// #1  Cleveland Cavaliers 45-28
// #2  Philadelphia 76ers 48-22
// #3  Memphis Grizzlies 43-27
// #4  Boston Celtics 49-23
```

The result is a string with all duplicate lines eliminated.

Discussion

First, we use split(/\r?\n/) to split the string at line breaks and create an array. This way, we can identify any duplicate elements in the array and eliminate them. We can achieve this by iterating over the array items, or more conveniently, by utilizing the Set constructor.

So we pass the array to Set(): it automatically eliminates duplicate items and returns a Set object containing unique values. Afterward, we apply the spread (...) syntax within an array to transform the Set back into an array again. Finally, we use join("\n") to concatenate all of the elements in the array with each element separated with a line break character.

It's possible to use this approach to remove duplicate lines that appear next to each other as well; however, the regex solution explained in the previous recipe would be much faster. On the other hand, the non-regex approach described in this recipe is faster than regex for removing duplicates that are separated by other lines.

Removing Duplicate Spaces

Task

Suppose you have a website with a blog section that allows guest posts. As a reviewer, you have noticed a common mistake in the submitted posts: double spaces between words. To address this issue, you want to create a function that automatically identifies and corrects this error by replacing double spaces with a single space.

A quick and dirty way to convert double spaces to a single space is to use the replaceAll() method like this:

```
part_3/removing_dup_spaces/removing_dup_spaces_ex1.js
const str = "A  day  without sunshine is like, you know, night.";

str.replaceAll("  ", " ");
// → "A day without sunshine is like, you know, night."
```

The first argument you pass to replaceAll() is the pattern to be replaced by the second argument. While replaceAll() is effective at converting double spaces to single spaces, it fails in cases where there are more than two spaces between words:

```
part_3/removing_dup_spaces/removing_dup_spaces_ex2.js
const str = "A        day without sunshine is like, you know, night.";

str.replaceAll("  ", " ");
// → "A    day without sunshine is like, you know, night."
```

You need a solution that can replace repeated spaces, not just double spaces.

Solution

Split the input string by space, store the resulting substrings in an array, remove any empty array items, and then combine the remaining elements using a single space:

part_3/removing_dup_spaces/removing_dup_spaces_ex3.js

```javascript
function replaceRepeatedSpaces(str) {
  return str.split(" ").filter(i=>i).join(" ");
}

const str = "A        day without sunshine is like, you know, night.";

replaceRepeatedSpaces(str);
// → "A day without sunshine is like, you know, night."
```

This code takes a string and removes any instances of consecutive spaces, then returns the modified string with a single space character between each word.

Discussion

In this function, we take a string and split it into an array of individual words using the split(" ") method. We then use the filter(i => i) method to remove any empty or falsy values from the resulting array. The filter() method creates a new array containing all the elements of the original array that pass a certain condition defined by a callback function.

Remember that the callback function needs to return either true or false. In this case, we're using the arrow function to just return the value from the array itself. Since an empty string is falsy, it is implicitly converted to false and gets removed from the array.

What Are Truthy and Falsy Values?

Truthy values are those that are considered true when evaluated as a Boolean, while falsy values are considered false. Here are the values considered falsy in JavaScript:

- 0 - The number zero
- 0n - The BigInt zero
- "" - An empty string
- null - Represents the absence of any value
- undefined - Represents an undefined value
- NaN - Stands for "Not a Number" and represents an invalid or unrepresentable value

All other values, including non-empty strings, non-zero numbers, arrays, objects, and functions, are considered truthy.

After filtering, we are left with an array of words that we can join together using a single space. If you need to process a large amount of text, using regex can be slightly faster than using JavaScript's methods. However, for most other cases, the performance difference is minimal.

Here's an example of how to implement the solution using regex:

```
function replaceRepeatedSpaces(str) {
  return str.replace(/ +/g," ");
}

const str = "A        day without sunshine is like, you know, night.";

replaceRepeatedSpaces(str);
// → "A day without sunshine is like, you know, night."
```

It's important to keep in mind that this recipe replaces only space characters and not all whitespace characters. A space character is what you get when you press the spacebar on your keyboard, while a whitespace character can represent a space, tab, new line, form feed, carriage return, or other similar characters. So, although a space character is a type of whitespace character, there are various other types of whitespace characters.

When it comes to replacing whitespace characters, using regex can be a better option because it's more concise. You'll learn more about whitespace characters in the next recipe.

Recipe 62

Removing Duplicate Whitespaces

Task

Suppose you discover that the guest posts on your blog site contain not just extra space characters, but also other whitespace characters, like tabs. So, this time, you want to replace all whitespace characters, including space, tab (\t), line feed (\n), carriage return (\r), vertical tab (\v), form feed (\f), and others.

For instance, consider the following string, where the space between "My" and "life" is made up of two tab characters. You can confirm the presence of a tab character by searching for \t in the string:

```
part_3/removing_dup_whitespaces/removing_dup_whitespaces_ex1.js
const str = " My                 life needs editing.";

/My\t\t/.test(str);      // → true
```

You need a solution that allows you to find repeated tabs or other whitespace characters and replace them with a single space.

Solution

Use a \s character class to match a whitespace character, then use a \s again to match any extra whitespaces that come after the first one:

```
part_3/removing_dup_whitespaces/removing_dup_whitespaces_ex2.js
const str = " My                 life needs editing.";

function removeExtraWhitespaces(str) {
  const re = /\s\s+/g;
  return str.replace(re, " ");
}

removeExtraWhitespaces(str);
// → " My life needs editing."
```

This function's purpose is to replace all instances of repeated whitespace characters (two or more) with a single space character. Notice the single whitespace at the beginning of the output. To ensure that the function also removes any additional leading/trailing whitespaces, you should apply trim() before returning the output string:

```
part_3/removing_dup_whitespaces/removing_dup_whitespaces_ex3.js
const str = " My                 life needs editing.";

function removeExtraWhitespaces(str) {
  const re = /\s\s+/g;
  str = str.replace(re, " ");
  str = str.trim();
  return str;
}

removeExtraWhitespaces(str);
// → "My life needs editing."
```

Mission accomplished!

Discussion

In JavaScript, "space" and "whitespace" are not the same thing. A space character is what you get when you press the spacebar on your keyboard. But a whitespace character is a broader term that includes any character that represents a blank area in text. It's important to understand the difference between these two types of characters because they can have different effects on your code.

The solution in this recipe replaces any type of whitespace character, so if a line feed (\n) comes after a tab (\t), they both get replaced by a space. If your intention is to replace only a specific type of whitespace character, then the following alternate recipe may be more suitable for your needs.

The Negated Form of \s

Remember, when using \S with a capital letter, it functions as the negation or opposite of \s with a small letter. \S enables you to match any character that is not a whitespace.

Recipe 63

Replacing Duplicate Whitespaces with the Same Type

Task

Imagine that your whitespace removal script is effective for paragraphs and headings, but you come across posts that have redundant tabs before certain list items, like this:

```
My list:
                1. Item one
        2. Item two
        3. Item three
```

If you implement the solution in the preceding recipe, the repeated tab characters will be replaced with a single space character, resulting in an inconsistent appearance of the items in the list:

```
My list:
 1. Item one
        2. Item two
        3. Item three
```

You need a solution that replaces repeated whitespaces with the same type of whitespace.

Solution

Capture the repeated whitespace with a capturing group and reference it with $1:

part_3/removing_dup_whitespaces_same_type/removing_dup_whitespaces_ex1.js

```
const str =
`My list:
                1. Item one
        2. Item two
        3. Item three`;

function removeExtraWhitespaces(str) {
  const re = /(\s)\1+/g;
  return str.replace(re, "$1");
}

removeExtraWhitespaces(str);
//"My list:
//      1. Item one
//      2. Item two
//      3. Item three"
```

This function replaces duplicate whitespaces with a single whitespace of the same type.

Discussion

In this recipe, str holds a list of items where each item is indented with a tab character (\t). The first item, however, has an extra tab character that we want to remove. Inside the function, we use (\s)\1+ to match any whitespace character followed by one or more occurrences of the same whitespace character.

Because we want to replace all these tab characters with a single tab character, we use a backreference to match the same character that was matched by the capturing group (\s).

Then, we use the special replacement pattern $1 to replace the matched characters with the same type of whitespace. The g flag at the end of the regular expression indicates global matching, meaning it will search for all occurrences of the pattern in the input string.

Extracting Text Enclosed in Double Quotes

Task

Suppose you have a movie review website, and you want to incorporate a mini-game widget into your page. The game prompts readers to guess the name of a celebrity based on a given nickname.

Your data source consists of a string that contains a list of celebrity names along with their corresponding nicknames, all enclosed in double quotation marks, like this:

```
1. Dwayne Johnson, also known as "The Rock"
2. Scarlett Johansson, also known as "Scarjo"
3. Bradley Cooper, also known as "Coop"
4. Jennifer Lawrence, also known as "Nitro"
5. Hugh Jackman, also known as "Sticks"
6. Tom Hardy, also known as "Weasel"
```

Your initial task is to extract the quoted texts from the string, so you can build an array of nicknames:

```
["The Rock", "Scarjo", "Coop", "Nitro", "Sticks", "Weasel"]
```

What you need is a way to detect a pair of quotation marks and extract the text within them.

Solution

Add double quotes to the beginning and end of a regex pattern, and use a negated character class to match characters that are not double quotes:

part_3/extracting_text_in_double_quotes/double_quoted_text_ex1.js
```
const str =
`1. Dwayne Johnson, also known as "The Rock"
2. Scarlett Johansson, also known as "Scarjo"
3. Bradley Cooper, also known as "Coop"
4. Jennifer Lawrence, also known as "Nitro"
5. Hugh Jackman, also known as "Sticks"
6. Tom Hardy, also known as "Weasel"`;
```

```
function extractQuotes(str) {
  const re = /"([^"]*)"/g;
  const quotes = [...str.matchAll(re)].map(value => value[1]);

  return quotes;
}
extractQuotes(str);
// → ["The Rock", "Scarjo", "Coop", "Nitro", "Sticks", "Weasel"]
```

This function returns an array of quoted text without including the quotes in the result.

Discussion

Double quotes don't have a special meaning in regular expressions, so we just add them to the pattern. Next, we use [^"] to match any character that's not double quotes, and append a * to repeat the class zero or more times. The pattern ends in a " to match the closing double quotes.

To retrieve the capturing groups of all matches, we use the matchAll() method. Because matchAll() returns an iterator, we can use the spread syntax (...) to unpack the object and generate an array from the outcome. This way we can use array methods on it.

Since we have a capturing group in the regex pattern, each match result contains an array with two elements: the entire matched substring and the content inside the quotes. By using value[1], we access the second element of the array, which corresponds to the content inside the quotes. Then we store them in the quotes array.

Matching a string enclosed in single quotes can be slightly more challenging as the text within the quotes may contain an apostrophe, such as in 'I can't.' The next recipe provides a solution for extracting text enclosed in single quotes.

Recipe 65

Extracting Text Enclosed in Single Quotes

Task

Suppose the data source for your mini-game widget lists the nicknames in single quotes rather than double quotes. Extracting the text within single quotes can be more challenging compared to double quotes because the nickname itself could contain an apostrophe.

For example:

```
Michael Eugene Archer, also known as 'D'Angelo'
```

You need a solution that can accurately identify a pair of single quotation marks while distinguishing them from an apostrophe.

Solution

Take advantage of lookarounds:

```
part_3/extracting_text_in_single_quotes/single_quoted_text_ex1.js
const str =
`1. Michael Eugene Archer, also known as 'D'Angelo'
2. Scarlett Johansson, also known as 'Scarjo'
3. Bradley Cooper, also known as 'Coop'
4. Jennifer Lawrence, also known as 'Nitro'
5. Hugh Jackman, also known as 'Sticks'
6. Tom Hardy, also known as 'Weasel'`;

function extractQuotes(str) {
  const re = /(?<!\w)'(.+?)'(?!\w)/g;
  const quotes = [...str.matchAll(re)].map(value => value[1]);

  return quotes;
}

extractQuotes(str);
// → ["D'Angelo", "Scarjo", "Coop", "Nitro", "Sticks", "Weasel"]
```

This solution allows you to capture single quoted strings that are not part of larger words or surrounded by other word characters.

Discussion

Let's examine the regex step by step:

```
/(?<!\w)'(.+?)'(?!\w)/
```

- (?<!\w) negative lookbehind: asserts that the regex inside does not match
  - \w matches any word character
- ' matches the character ' literally
- (.+?) 1st capturing group
  - . matches any character (except for line terminators)
  - +? matches the previous token between one and unlimited times, as few times as possible (lazy)
- ' matches the character ' literally
- (?!\w) negative lookahead: asserts that the regex inside does not match
  - \w matches any word character

The regex begins with a negative lookbehind to match an opening single quote that isn't preceded by a word character (a letter, a digit, or underscore). As a result, it won't match words like "What's." Next, (.+?) matches any character one or more times. The question mark makes the match *non-greedy*, which means the quantifier tries to match its preceding item as few times as possible (see Recipe 38, Creating Lazy Quantifiers with the Question Mark, on page 102). Without the question mark, the pattern would match the last closing quotation mark in the string.

Finally, '(?!\w) matches a single quote that's not followed by a word character—thanks to the negative lookahead.

Recipe 66

Escaping a String for Use in a Regex

Task

Imagine a scenario where you're designing a search feature for an online bookstore. Within the app's search functionality, there is a field where users can enter a partial title or author's name to find the specific book they are looking for.

Your code involves using the user-provided string as a component of a regex to search a database. In order to safeguard your app from potential attacks, you should implement a function that escapes all regex metacharacters in the user-provided string before using it as a component of your search pattern.

Escaping ensures that the special characters within the string are properly handled and do not inadvertently affect the behavior of the regular expression.

Solution

To ensure that characters with special meanings within a pattern are treated as ordinary characters without any special interpretation, you can create a function that adds a backslash before those characters:

part_3/escaping_metacharacters/escaping_ex1.js
```
function escapeRegex(str) {
  const re = /[-\\^$*+?.()|[\]{}]/g;
  return str.replace(re, "\\$&");
}

const str = "These should be escaped: - \\ ^ $ * + ? . ( ) | [ ] { }";
const escaped = escapeRegex(str);

console.log(escaped);
// → "These should be escaped: \- \\ \^ \$ \* \+ \? \. \( \) \| \[ \] \{ \}"
```

The string is now safe to use as part of your regex.

Discussion

The regex for this recipe encapsulates all the regex metacharacters in a character class. The square brackets [] denote a character class, which means any character within the class will be matched. Then, the replace() method replaces all occurrences of the metacharacters with their escaped versions.

The $& in the replacement string represents the matched substring itself. Notice the double backslash preceding it: since the backslash is used as the escape character, you cannot use it directly if you want to add a literal backslash to a string. Instead, you need to type two backslashes in a row. This is because the first backslash acts as an escape character for the second backslash, telling JavaScript to treat the second backslash as a literal character instead of an escape sequence.

Here's the reasoning behind escaping each of those characters in the character class:

- - The hyphen symbol defines a range of characters in a character class. To prevent accidental creation of ranges while incorporating text within a character class, it's necessary to escape it
- \ The backslash can be used to make certain literal characters special. For example, \n creates a newline character (rather than a backslash followed by the letter n)

- ^ The caret symbol matches the start of a line/string. It can also create a negated character class
- $ The dollar symbol matches the end of a line/string
- * The * quantifier matches its preceding item zero or more times
- + The + quantifier matches its preceding item one or more times
- ? The ? quantifier matches its preceding item zero or one time
- . The dot symbol matches any character
- | The vertical bar matches any of two or more options
- () Parentheses are used for capturing, grouping, and other constructs
- [] Square brackets create a character class
- {} Curly brackets create a quantifier

When using the pattern in this recipe, make sure to use the g flag to replace all matches, rather than only the first.

It's important to be careful when using user-provided input in your regex. Failing to do so could render your program vulnerable to a type of attack called *ReDos* (regular expression denial of service). An attacker could potentially exploit your program by providing an extremely intricate regex that requires a significant amount of time to process.

When evaluating user input in a browser, a ReDoS attack will typically cause the browser to hang. But, when the input is being evaluated on a server, the consequences can be more severe and potentially lead to a denial-of-service attack. In such an attack, the attacker floods the server with a barrage of highly processing-intensive requests, effectively preventing the server from servicing legitimate requests.

In this case, protecting your program from ReDoS isn't too difficult: escape all metacharacters that could alter the pattern of the expression. This can be done by placing a backslash before the metacharacter, which tells the regex engine to treat it as a literal character.

Escaping Metacharacters in Other Languages

There exist built-in functions in several programming languages that automatically escape regex metacharacters. For example, Java has Pattern.quote(str) and Python provides e.escape(str). If you're using the Lodash library, you might as well take advantage of its _.escapeRegExp() method to escape metacharacters.

Recipe 67

Striping Invalid Characters from Filenames

Task

Suppose you operate a file hosting service. To ensure a smooth download process, you should avoid certain characters in the filenames of the files being provided for download. In iOS and macOS, the filename cannot contain a colon (:), while Android and Windows OS have stricter restrictions and do not allow the use of <, >, :, ", /, \, |, ?, and * in filenames.

The reason is that the OS uses these characters for enclosing paths in quotes, marking off drives and directories, indicating wildcards and command line redirection, etc. Moreover, there are certain words that Windows uses as reserved names for internal purposes, and as a result, they cannot be used as filenames.

These reserved names are as follows:

```
LPT1, LPT2, LPT3, LPT4, LPT5, LPT6, LPT7, LPT8, LPT9,
COM1, COM2, COM3, COM4, COM5, COM6, COM7, COM8, COM9,
CON, PRN, AUX, NUL
```

When attempting to download a file with invalid characters in its name, Windows will automatically replace those characters with an underscore, without any warning to the user. To avoid such issues, you may want to create a script that can detect problematic characters in a filename and notify the user to resolve them before proceeding with the download.

Solution

To improve readability and maintainability, it's easier to test each list of characters and words separately, rather than merging them and using a single regex. Create a function that accepts a filename as an input, tests each regex against it, and returns true if the tests pass:

```
part_3/striping_invalid_characters/striping_ex1.js
let reservedNames =
`LPT1, LPT2, LPT3, LPT4, LPT5, LPT6, LPT7, LPT8, LPT9,
COM1, COM2, COM3, COM4, COM5, COM6, COM7, COM8, COM9,
CON, PRN, AUX, NUL`;

// Create an array from the reservedNames string
```

```
reservedNames = reservedNames.split(/,\s/);

function isValidFilename(name) {
  const re1 = new RegExp(`^(${reservedNames.join("|")})$`, "i");
  const re2 = /[<>:"/\\|?*]/;
  return !(re1.test(name) || re2.test(name));
}

isValidFilename("COM1");        // → false
isValidFilename("com1");        // → false
isValidFilename("com1_");       // → true
isValidFilename("@com1");       // → true
isValidFilename("]-:");         // → false
isValidFilename("<myfile>");    // → false
```

Success!

Discussion

To start with, prepare an array containing the invalid characters/names. If you're like me and don't feel like creating the array by typing, you can use the split() method to separate the reserved names and store them in the array. The result will be as follows:

```
let reservedNames =
`LPT1, LPT2, LPT3, LPT4, LPT5, LPT6, LPT7, LPT8, LPT9,
COM1, COM2, COM3, COM4, COM5, COM6, COM7, COM8, COM9,
CON, PRN, AUX, NUL`;

reservedNames.split(/,\s/);
// → ["LPT1", "LPT2", "LPT3", "LPT4", "LPT5", "LPT6", "LPT7", "LPT8", "LPT9",
// "COM1", "COM2", "COM3", "COM4", "COM5", "COM6", "COM7", "COM8", "COM9",
// "CON", "PRN", "AUX", "NUL"]
```

Inside the isValidFilename() function, we use the RegExp constructor to join the items of the resulting array with a pipe symbol to form alternations like this: LPT1|LPT2|LPT3...

If you want to avoid creating the pattern dynamically, you don't have to type each name separately. Instead, take advantage of a character class to define a range:

```
/^(LPT[1-9]|COM[1-9]|CON|PRN|AUX|NUL)$/i
```

A filename with these words is invalid only if it doesn't contain additional characters. For example, "LPT1" is an invalid filename, but not "LPT1z" or "ALPT1." The caret symbol (^) at the start of the pattern asserts the beginning of the string and ensures that no other characters precede the desired string match. Similarly, the dollar symbol ($) asserts the end of the string.

The second pattern, which lists reserved characters, consists of only nine characters. So, it's sufficient to include them in a character class using square brackets []. A character class matches any single character that appears between the brackets, so we can check if any of those characters exist in the given string.

Inside character classes, the backslash is considered a metacharacter and, therefore, requires escaping with another backslash. But, all other characters are treated as literal characters.

Filenames may contain characters that are not allowed by the operating system or filesystem. By using a regex pattern, we can detect those characters and provide a problem-free download process.

Recipe 68

Matching Floating-Point Numbers

Task

Suppose you aim to write a regex to match floating-point values because you want to extract stock prices from a string. Or perhaps you want to retrieve other values that have a floating-point representation, such as interest rates, sensor readings, temperatures, or coordinates (latitude and longitude).

You want to be able to specify whether the presence of the sign, integer, and fraction components is mandatory or optional. The regex to use depends on the optional components of the floating-point number. Therefore, this recipe offers different patterns as potential solutions.

Solution

Matching a floating-point value that has a sign, integer, and fraction components:

```
[+-]\d+\.\d+
```

Matching a floating-point value that may have an optional sign, but must have integer and fraction components:

```
[+-]?\d+\.\d+
```

Matching a floating-point value with optional sign and integer but mandatory fraction:

```
[+-]?\d*\.\d+
```

Example:

Let's extract the first floating-point number that appears in a string. The value may have an optional sign, but must have integer and fraction components:

```
part_3/matching_floating_points/fp_ex1.js
function extractFloatingPoint(str) {
  const re = /[+-]?\d+\.\d+/;
  return str.match(re)[0];
}

extractFloatingPoint("It's -4.19 today.");
// → "-4.19"
```

Mission accomplished!

Discussion

In the first pattern, we use square brackets to create a character class that matches either a plus sign (+) or a minus sign (-), followed by one or more digits (\d+), followed by a literal period (.), followed by one or more digits again (\d+). This matches a floating point numbering a question mark after the character class. Similarly, replacing the plus sign with an asterisk in the integer digits repetition allows for zero or more digits instead of one or more.

In the example, we're verifying if a floating-point number exists within a larger body of text. But, if you want to verify whether the entire input is a floating-point number, you should use the ^ and $ boundaries.

Recipe 69

Matching Formatted Numbers with Thousand Separators

Task

Suppose you are developing a price comparison app to assist users in comparing product or service prices across various online retailers. Since prices often include thousand separators, you find yourself in need of a regex pattern that can accurately detect numbers with thousand separators.

So, if a website lists the product like this:

```
Great deal! $7,499 %20 Price drop
```

Your regex should be able to extract 7,499.

Solution

To extract numbers with thousand separators, you can use this function:

part_3/matching_thousand_separators/matching_thousand_separators_ex1.js
```
function extractNumbers(str) {
  const re = /\d{1,3}(?:,\d{3})*(?:\.\d+)?/g;
  return str.match(re)[0];
}

extractNumbers("Great deal! $7,499 %20 Price drop");
// → "7,499"
```

The regex pattern in this code matches numbers that use the comma as the thousand separator and the dot as the decimal separator. Matching the fraction part is optional, but if the fraction is not present, then the decimal point should not be included.

Discussion

Numbers with a large number of digits are often separated into groups using a delimiter like a comma or a period—to make them easier to read. Typically, English-speaking countries use commas as the delimiter, such as 20,000, while European countries use periods or spaces, like 20.000 or 20 000.

The pattern in this recipe starts by matching a sequence of 1 to 3 digits, succeeded by a group that matches zero or more occurrences of a comma followed by three digits. The combination of these two patterns matches any number with one or more groups of three digits separated by commas. To allow the fraction part to be optional, we just add a question mark after the group.

Let's examine the regex pattern step by step:

```
/\d{1,3}(?:,\d{3})*(?:\.\d+)?/
```

- \d matches a digit
  - {1,3} matches the previous token between 1 and 3 times

- `(?:,\d{3})` non-capturing group
  - ○ `,` matches the comma character literally
  - ○ `\d` matches a digit
    - ○ `{3}` matches the previous token exactly 3 times
- `*` matches the previous token zero or more times
- `(?:\.\d+)?` non-capturing group
  - ○ `\.` matches the period character literally
  - ○ `\d` matches a digit
    - ○ `+` matches the previous token one or more times
- `?` matches the previous token zero or one time

Here are some examples of numbers that would match this pattern:

```
1
100
1,000
10,000
100,000
1,000,000
1,000,000.00 (decimal point after the thousands separator)
```

And here are some examples of numbers that would not correctly match:

```
1.000.000 (decimal point instead of comma)
1,00 (incorrect grouping of digits)
10,0 (incorrect grouping of digits)
```

To match numbers that use periods instead of commas as thousand separators, we need to slightly adjust the pattern. Replace the comma in the second group with a period and the period in the third group with a comma:

part_3/matching_thousand_separators/matching_thousand_separators_ex2.js
```
function extractNumbers(str) {
  const re = /\d{1,3}(?:\.\d{3})*(?:,\d+)?/g;
  return str.match(re)[0];
}

extractNumbers("For sale €1.499.000 3 beds 4 baths");
// → "1.499.000"
```

This function allows us to match the thousand separators used in countries such as Germany, Greece, and Italy. If you want to add thousand separators to numbers, you can take advantage of the intl.numberformat() constructor discussed in Recipe 15, Adding Thousand Separators to Numbers with Intl.NumberFormat(), on page 36.

Matching Nearby Words

Task

Suppose you want to search for the term "client-side" in a tutorial database because you've been asked to assess whether client-side issues are sufficiently covered for new hires. If you write a regex that matches only the exact word, it would be unable to retrieve results for instances that contain the words "client" and "side" without being adjacent to each other. For example, tutorials with phrases such as "client- and server-side" or "client and server side" would not be included in the search results.

But if you specify a proximity search for the words, where they appear within a certain number of characters of each other, it will help you to find more relevant results. So, what you need is to create a pattern that can locate words, as long as they appear within a specific distance of each other.

Solution

To find words near each other, use the following function:

```
part_3/proximity_search/proximity_search_ex1.js
function findNearbyWords(text, word1, word2, maxDistance) {
  const regex = new RegExp(`${word1}.{0,${maxDistance}}${word2}`, "gi");
  const matches = text.match(regex);
  return matches;
}

const text = "Both client- and server-side scripts must validate form data.";
const word1 = "client";
const word2 = "side";
const maxDistance = 20;

findNearbyWords(text, word1, word2, maxDistance);
// → ["client- and server-side"]
```

This function performs a proximity search for "client" and "side" within 20 characters of each other and retrieves the part of the string that contains them.

Discussion

We construct the pattern by using a template literal that contains the word1 and word2 variables, as well as the maxDistance variable as a quantifier {0,${maxDistance}} to match between word1 and word2. Note that ${word1}, ${maxDistance}, and ${word2} are JavaScript placeholders for performing substitutions, and they are entirely distinct from the regex syntax. Let's take a closer look:

```
${word1}.{0,${maxDistance}}${word2}
```

- ${word1} gets replaced with "client"
- . matches any character that is not a line break character
  - {0,${maxDistance}} gets replaced with {0,20}, so it matches the previous token between 0 to 20 times
- ${word2} gets replaced with "side"

Additionally, we add the g and i flags to the regex to make it global and case-insensitive. Then, we call the match() method on the text with the regex object as an argument. The output will be an array of matches that contain word1 and word2 within maxDistance characters of each other.

Proximity search techniques can be especially useful when searching for complex or technical information. By specifying that we want to see results where certain words or phrases appear near each other, we can find the text we're looking for more accurately.

Recipe 71

Highlighting Sentences Containing a Specific Word

Task

Suppose you aim to add a search feature to your program that highlights all sentences in a text containing a specific word. For example, you are comparing a translated book to the original text, which uses a word with multiple meanings. You need to see not only the word, but the context in which it is used to help check that the proper translation was used.

While finding the word using regex is relatively straightforward, identifying the sentence in which it appears is a bit more challenging. To highlight the sentence containing the specified word found in a text, you should write a pattern capable of differentiating between one sentence and another.

Solution

Start with writing the JavaScript component, which comprises two primary functions: highlight() and unhighlight(). The highlight() function retrieves the search value entered in an HTML input and applies a regex that identifies the sentence encompassing the search term. By encasing the matched sentence with <mark></mark> tags, you can accomplish your objective:

part_3/highlighting_sentences/highlight_ex1.js

```
Line 1   const el = document.querySelector("#string");

         function highlight() {

    5       // Get the value of #input
           const keyword = document.querySelector("#input").value;

           // If the input is empty don't execute the rest of the function
           if(keyword === "") {
   10        return;
           }

           // Remove any existing highlights from the text
           unhighlight();
   15
           // Construct a regular expression
           const re = new RegExp(`([^.!?]*\\b${keyword}\\b[^.!?]*.?)`, "gi");

           // Wrap each sentence in a pair of <mark></mark> tags
   20      el.innerHTML = el.innerHTML.replace(re,"<mark>$1</mark>");
         }

         function unhighlight() {

   25      // Construct a regex that matches <mark> and </mark> tags
           const re = /<\/?mark>/g;

           // Remove tags by replacing each tag with an empty string
           el.innerHTML = el.innerHTML.replace(re, "");
   30    }

         document.querySelector("#highlight").addEventListener("click", highlight);
         document.querySelector("#unhighlight").addEventListener("click", unhighlight);
```

Now, create two HTML buttons: one to initiate highlighting and another to reverse the effect. You also need an input field to type in a search keyword:

```
<button id="highlight">Highlight All</button>
<button id="unhighlight">Unhighlight</button>
<input id="input" type="text" value="crocodiles">
```

The input element has a default value of "crocodiles." If you don't want any text to appear in the input when the page loads, you can remove the value property. To keep things simple, let's limit the text we want to search to a few sentences:

```
part_3/highlighting_sentences/highlight_ex1.html
<!doctype html>
<html lang="en-us">
<head>
  <meta charset="utf-8">
  <meta name="viewport" content="width=device-width, initial-scale=1">
  <script src="highlight_ex1.js" defer></script>
</head>
<body>
  <p id="string">
  Crocodiles are like giant lizards with a serious attitude problem. They're
  like the grumpy old men of the animal kingdom, constantly scowling and
  grunting like they've got a bad case of indigestion. But despite their
  intimidating demeanor, crocodiles do have a soft side. Just try playing
  them some smooth jazz or offering them a plate of freshly baked cookies
  —they'll be putty in your hands. All in all, crocodiles are just
  misunderstood creatures in need of a little love and a good chiropractor.
  </p>

  <button id="highlight">Highlight All</button>
  <button id="unhighlight">Unhighlight</button>
  <input id="input" type="text" value="crocodiles">
</body>

</html>
```

Fantastic! The code now highlights every sentence in the text that includes a particular term.

Discussion

In the JavaScript code, we define two functions and two event listeners. The first function, highlight(), is executed when the user clicks the "highlight" button. Inside the function, we first retrieve the user's input value and store it in a variable called keyword. If the input is empty, we terminate the function without doing anything. If the input is not empty, we call unhighlight() to remove any existing highlights in the HTML element.

Next, we create a regex pattern that matches any sentence containing the keyword. We use the negated character class [^.!?] to match a single character that is not a dot, exclamation point, or question mark. This allows us to differentiate between one sentence and another. If you want the pattern to identify sentences that end with other punctuation marks, such as a colon, you can include them in the character class.

Notice Line 17, where we create an instance of the RegExp object instead of a regular expression literal. This is essential because we want to dynamically insert the text from the HTML input into the regex pattern. We also need to use backticks to delimit the pattern instead of double or single quotes. Without backticks, the ${keyword} placeholder wouldn't function as intended.

Pay attention to the presence of the backslash before the word boundary (\b). Because we're using the word boundary in a RegExp object, it's necessary to escape it with a backslash.

The following is how the regex engine perceives the pattern:

```
([^.!?]*\\b${keyword}\\b[^.!?]*.?)
```

- ([^.!?]*\\b${keyword}\\b[^.!?]*.?) 1st capturing group
  - [^.!?] matches any character that isn't ., !, or ?
    - * matches zero or more sequences of the preceding item
  - \\b asserts a word boundary
  - ${keyword} inserts the value of the keyword constant into the pattern
  - \\b asserts a word boundary
  - [^.!?] matches any character that isn't ., !, or ?
    - * matches zero or more sequences of the preceding item
  - . matches any character that's not a line break character
    - ? matches zero or one occurrence of the preceding item
- Flags
  - g tells the regex engine to match all occurrences rather than stopping after the first match
  - i makes the search case-insensitive

At the end of the function, we use the replace() method to replace all matches of the pattern with the matched string surrounded by <mark></mark>. There are various ways in HTML to denote text that holds significance. In this case, we have opted for the <mark> element, which instructs the web browser to emphasize the enclosed text by highlighting it in yellow.

The second function, unhighlight(), is called when the user clicks the "unhighlight" button. It simply creates a regex pattern that matches any <mark> or </mark> tags in the HTML, and then removes those tags using the replace() method. The last two lines of code add the respective event listeners to the "highlight" and "unhighlight" buttons. When each button is clicked, the corresponding function is executed.

Being cautious while using the input submitted by the user in your regex is crucial. If you don't verify the input, your program could become vulnerable to a potential attack known as *ReDoS*. To learn about safeguarding your application from such attacks, see Recipe 66, Escaping a String for Use in a Regex, on page 169.

Recipe 72

Highlighting Text in Real Time

Task

Suppose you want to add a search functionality to your application that behaves similarly to Google Chrome's "find in page" tool. With this feature, as the user types their search query into the search field, Chrome highlights the corresponding text on the page in real time. This enables users to quickly locate the information they are searching for without having to manually scan the entire page.

Solution

Define an HTML page with an input element and a div element containing some text. The input element should have an ID of "search-input," and the div element should have an ID of "search-results":

```
part_3/highlighting_in_realtime/highlighting_in_realtime_ex1.html
<!DOCTYPE html>
<html>
<head>
  <script src="highlighting_in_realtime_ex1.js" defer></script>
</head>
<body>
  <input type="text" id="search-input" placeholder="Search...">
  <div id="search-results">Snakes are quite the characters. Have you seen
  their fashion sense? It's all stripes and scales, like they're trying to
  be both a zebra and a dragon at the same time. But don't let their smooth
  moves fool you—snakes can be quite hiss-terical when they want to be.
  </div>
</body>
</html>
```

Now, create the JavaScript code that takes the input and highlights the text:

```
part_3/highlighting_in_realtime/highlighting_in_realtime_ex1.js
const searchInput = document.querySelector("#search-input");
const searchResults = document.querySelector("#search-results");
const content = searchResults.innerHTML;

function highlightText() {
  const searchText = searchInput.value.trim().toLowerCase();

  if (searchText.length > 0) {
    const searchRegex = new RegExp(searchText, "gi");
    const highlightedText = content.replace(searchRegex, "<mark>$&</mark>");

    searchResults.innerHTML = highlightedText;
  } else {
    searchResults.innerHTML = content;
  }
}

searchInput.addEventListener("input", highlightText);
```

This code creates a live search functionality that highlights all occurrences of the search term in the "search-results" div element as the user types in the input field.

Discussion

The JavaScript code starts by creating references to the input, div, and the content of the div element. We add an event listener to the input element using the addEventListener() method. The event listener listens for changes to the input value and triggers the highlightText() function when the input changes.

Inside highlightText(), we retrieve the value entered into the searchInput element, remove any leading or trailing whitespace characters, convert the remaining string value to lowercase, and store the result in the searchText variable.

Next, we check if the length of searchText is greater than zero. If so, we create a regex object using the given input. We also pass the g and i flags as the second parameter to indicate that the regex should match all occurrences globally and be case-insensitive.

Using the replace() method on the content variable, we replace all occurrences of the search text with the same text wrapped in an HTML <mark> tag. Finally, we update the innerHTML property of the searchResults element to display the highlighted text.

If the length of searchText is zero, we set the innerHTML property to the original content variable, which displays the text as it was initially. This step is essential because if the user deletes the entire search term, the text shouldn't have highlights anymore.

Users are increasingly expecting interactive and dynamic interfaces that respond to their actions in real time. One such feature that has become popular is real-time text highlighting. Take advantage of it to make it easier for your users to find the information they need.

Protecting Your App from ReDoS Attacks

⚠ Be careful when reusing the text provided by the user in your regex pattern. If you fail to sanitize the text properly, your app may become vulnerable to ReDoS attacks. To learn more, see Recipe 66, Escaping a String for Use in a Regex, on page 169.

Recipe 73

Converting Plain Text into HTML-Ready Markup

Task

Imagine you intend to display the text entered by users on a web page. A frustrating aspect of web programming is the lack of compatibility between HTML and plain text, despite their frequent interchangeable use. While people may enter information in plain text format in the text areas of forms, it's likely that you'd want to display the same information in HTML format. To illustrate, consider this example, where a user has entered a question on a forum page:

```
Hey guys,

I need your help with something urgent. My cat, Mr. Whiskers, has been acting
super weird lately. He won't stop meowing, he keeps knocking down my plants,
and to top it off, he's been stealing my socks.

Do you know of any good cat therapists that you can recommend?

Thanks
```

If you don't include <br> or <p> tags to indicate line breaks in the markup, the resulting appearance when loaded into a web browser will be like this:

```
Hey guys, I need your help with something urgent. My cat, Mr. Whiskers,
has been acting super weird lately. He won't stop meowing, he keeps knocking
```

down my plants, and to top it off, he's been stealing my socks. Do you know
of any good cat therapists that you can recommend? Thanks

What you need is a solution that adds relevant HTML tags to paragraphs.

Solution

Search for newline characters in the supplied text and replace them with
HTML tags:

part_3/converting_text_to_html/text_to_html_ex1.js

```
function convertTextToHTML(str) {

  // Replace newline characters with <br>
  str = str.replace(/\r\n|\n/g, "<br>");

  // Replace two consecutive <br> with </p><p>
  str = str.replace(/<br>\s*<br>/g, "</p><p>");

  // Enclose the entire string in <p></p>
  str = `<p>${str}</p>`;
  return str;
}

const str =
`Hey guys,

I need your help with something urgent. My cat, Mr. Whiskers, has been acting
super weird lately. He won't stop meowing, he keeps knocking down my plants,
and to top it off, he's been stealing my socks.

Do you know of any good cat therapists that you can recommend?

Thanks
`;

convertTextToHTML(str);
// → <p>Hey guys, </p><p>I need your help with something urgent. My cat, Mr.
// Whiskers, has been acting <br>super weird lately. He won't stop meowing,
// he keeps knocking down my plants, <br>and to top it off, he's been
// stealing my socks. </p><p>Do you know of any good cat therapists that you
// can recommend?</p><p>Thanks<br></p>"
```

Now, with the HTML tags added, the text will be displayed properly in the
browser.

Discussion

Reusing the text provided by the user without sanitizing it is unwise because
it leaves the system vulnerable to XSS attacks. But, for this recipe, let's

overlook this concern and assume that the input is safe to use (if you want to learn how to protect against XSS attacks, check out the link in the foot-note.[5])

We first use the regex /\r\n|\n/g to find newline characters that are used in Microsoft Windows/DOS (\r\n) or Unix and Unix-like systems (\n). And we replace them with <br>.

In order to format paragraphs in HTML, it's necessary to enclose them within <p></p> tags. One way to achieve this is to identify any instance of two con-secutive line breaks and replace them with </p><p> (Line 7).

Finally, we wrap the complete string with <p></p> tags and then return the resulting string. Before using this function to convert text to HTML, you may want to replace &, <, >, ", and ' characters with HTML entities to prevent browsers from interpreting HTML tags entered by users (see Recipe 8, Con-verting HTML Markup to HTML Entities with replaceAll(), on page 18).

Wrapping Up

When working with regex, it's not uncommon to encounter situations where your pattern fails to work as expected. Tracking down and fixing errors in regex can be a systematic process. Let's quickly go over some strategies to assist you in troubleshooting and resolving issues when your pattern isn't working as intended:

- Understand the regex flavor: the regex pattern you come across on the internet may be tailored to a particular regex engine. Before incorporating it into your code, ensure that it works with the JavaScript regex flavor, or use a tool for conversion.

- Break it down: if your pattern is complex, try breaking it down into smaller parts and testing each part separately. This allows you to isolate the problematic section and identify where the issue lies.

- Be aware of special characters and escaping: ensure that special charac-ters are properly escaped if needed. Special characters such as dot (.), asterisk (*), plus (+), question mark (?), brackets ([]), and others have special meanings and require escaping with a backslash to match them literally.

---

5.   https://www.acunetix.com/websitesecurity/cross-site-scripting/#:~:text=In%20a%20Cross%2Dsite%20Script-ing,vulnerable%20to%20Cross%2Dsite%20scripting.

- Verify the placement of capturing groups: when using capturing groups, check if they are correctly defined and capture the intended content. Incorrect grouping can lead to unexpected results or failed matches.

- Test data: evaluate the data you are applying the regex pattern to. Verify that it matches the format and content you expect.

- Use regex testing tools: a good regex tool allows you to test your regex pattern in real time, provides detailed error messages, highlights issues with the pattern, and gives explanations for failed matches. For a selection of tools, see Appendix 3, Testing Regex with Specialized Tools, on page 203.

When making a decision on whether to use a regex or an alternative solution, two main factors come into play: performance and maintainability. Regular expressions can be computationally expensive, especially when dealing with large inputs or complex patterns. If performance is a critical factor for your task, and regex is causing performance issues, you might need to consider alternative solutions, such as string manipulation functions or specialized parsing libraries.

To identify if a regex is causing performance problems for your app, measure the execution time of your code. You can use built-in timing functions or performance profiling tools. Compare the execution time with and without the regex to see if there is a significant difference.

If you have identified that the regex is the culprit, consider optimizing it before searching for an alternative solution. Look for opportunities to simplify or refactor the regex pattern. For example, try to eliminate unnecessary capturing groups and use more specific expressions whenever possible.

Another consideration is whether your code will be maintained by others. Regular expressions can become convoluted and hard to understand, particularly for complex patterns. So, opting for a more explicit solution might be preferable. It's essential to weigh the trade-offs and choose the most appropriate solution based on the specific requirements of your project.

Text processing is a fundamental aspect of modern computing and plays an essential role in many applications such as natural language processing, machine learning, information retrieval, and data analysis. In this book, we have explored both traditional and state-of-the-art approaches to text processing in JavaScript.

As technology continues to advance, the demand for effective text-processing techniques will only grow. I hope this book has provided you with the foundational knowledge and practical skills needed to meet this demand.

May I Request a Favor from You?

Thank you for taking the time to read this book. May I request a favor? Could you spare a minute to write a brief comment about this book on Amazon or Goodreads? Your feedback is incredibly valuable, not just to me as an author, but to potential readers as well. I make it a point to read all reviews and greatly appreciate sincere feedback. To me, the true reward for my efforts is the knowledge that I'm making a positive impact on the JavaScript community.

Thanks again, and I really look forward to reading your feedback!

What Is Unicode?

Throughout this book, you'll encounter the word "Unicode" in several recipes. So, what exactly is Unicode?

Unicode is a character encoding system that provides a consistent way of encoding, processing, and displaying written texts. Put simply, an encoding system assigns numbers to characters, which can then be translated into binary language used by computers.

Unicode is implemented in all modern operation systems and programming languages. And it plays an increasingly important role in the JavaScript language. Prior to the invention of Unicode, there were hundreds of different character encoding systems, most of which were severely limited in size and scope and incompatible with one another.

The most widely used character encoding system besides Unicode is ASCII. American Standard Code for Information Interchange (ASCII) was published in 1963 as a standard for electronic communication. ASCII is based on a seven-bit byte, with each byte representing a character, capable of encoding 128 characters, including lowercase letters a-z, uppercase letters A-Z, digits 0-9, and punctuation symbols.

In addition, 33 non-printing control signals are set aside for Teletype machines, most of which are now obsolete. Because ASCII is an American standard designed for transmitting English characters, it cannot represent characters from other languages. As computers became more prevalent in other parts of the world, other encoding systems were invented to represent characters in other languages.

Over time, the need to support new languages led to the creation of hundreds of conflicting ways to encode characters. These encoding systems were not only inconsistent but also incomplete: two encodings could encode the same character using different codes, and they were only able to encode a small number of characters.

Unicode aims to solve this problem by unifying all existing character encoding systems and replacing them with a universal character encoding standard supporting every character in every writing system and language in the world. By providing a standard to encode multilingual text, Unicode creates the foundation for developing global software.

Prior to the introduction of the Unicode standard, most programs supported a small set of encodings. They were designed primarily for larger markets due to the cost and complexity of developing specific versions of programs for smaller markets. Furthermore, converting text between different programs posed a risk of corruption. Unicode's ability to easily exchange text data internationally enables programs to function anywhere in the world.

To achieve this, Unicode uses more bits to encode each character, allowing more space for encoding. At this time, the most recent version of the Unicode standard, Unicode 15.0, contains a collection of 149,186 characters from many modern and historic scripts.

In addition to including modern and classical forms of many languages from around the world, the standard contains important symbol sets, including punctuation marks, mathematics symbols, currency symbols, technical symbols, emojis, dingbats, and geometric shapes.

With a capacity of over one million characters, Unicode is more than enough for encoding text expressed in most writing systems. But, capacity limitation in fonts means no one font set supports all Unicode characters. So even though Unicode provides a way to display the characters, they still won't display right if they are not part of the font being used.

The reason behind this is that a font can only have 16 bits of glyph identifiers, which corresponds to 65,536 glyphs (note that a glyph is different from a character[1]). As a result, it has been technically impossible to represent all +149,186 characters of Unicode with a single font.

Characters in Unicode are represented in three encoding forms:

- 8-bit form (UTF-8)
- 16-bit form (UTF-16)
- 32-bit form (UTF-32)

---

1.   https://help.fontlab.com/fontlab/7/manual/About-Glyphs/

UTF is the abbreviation for Unicode Transformation Format, and the number following it indicates the number of bits used to encode each character. The 8-bit form of Unicode is the most common character encoding on the web. It was designed not only to represent standard Unicode characters but also to be backward compatible with ASCII. The ASCII characters are the first 128 code points in Unicode (UTF-8).

Therefore, an ASCII text is also considered a Unicode text. In fact, Unicode is a superset of all characters in common use today because it includes characters from various international standards, as well as important industry character sets. UTF-16 represents characters using one or two 16-bit integers. Most of the characters in major languages can be represented using one 16-bit code unit.

These characters, known as Basic Multilingual Plane (BMP), are encoded in the first 65,536 code points and require 2 bytes per character. Any character beyond BMP is called a supplementary character and cannot be represented in just 16 bits. Supplementary characters need a pair of 16-bit surrogate code units and are encoded in 4 bytes. Unicode allocates 2,048 code points as surrogate code points for the UTF-16 form.

For UTF-8, 1 byte is used to represent characters in ASCII, 3 bytes for the rest of the BMP, and 4 bytes for supplementary characters. UTF-32 is a fixed-width encoding using 4 bytes for all characters — unlike UTF-8 and UTF-16, which represent each code point by a variable number of code values.

Unicode code points are usually represented in hexadecimal notation and prefixed with U+. The range between U+0000 and U+FFFF represents code points in BMP. For supplementary characters, five or six hex digits are used to represent code points, and the range is between U+10000 and U+10FFFF.

The characters you see on computers are actually binary data consisting of a series of ones and zeros. A character encoding interprets those binary data into real characters. In order to accomplish this, the encoding associates each character with a number which is called a code point. For example, the character "F" is assigned a code point of U+0046.

A character that's assigned to a specific code point is called an encoded character. In JavaScript, you can use the code point of a character directly by preceding the code point with \u, as in this example:

```
console.log("\u0046");    // → F
```

A character encoding has two components: an encoder and a decoder. When you input text, the encoder translates the characters into a sequence of numeric values (bytes) that represents those characters. To display the characters, the decoder translates the sequence of bytes back into characters.

Since ES2015, you can use most Unicode characters as an identifier. For example:

```
appendix/unicode/unicode_ex1.js
// An identifier in the Persian language
let سلام = "hi";
console.log(سلام);     // → hi

// An identifier in the Japanese language
let こんにちは = "Hello";
console.log(こんにちは);        // → Hello
```

The goal of Unicode is to enable everybody in the world to use their language on computers. Therefore, it's no wonder Unicode is the most used character set encoding in the world.

If you are interested in reading more about Unicode, check out unicode.org.[2]

---

2.   https://home.unicode.org/

Implementing Regex in JavaScript

There are several ways to implement regular expressions in JavaScript. In this book, we've mostly worked with test(), match(), and replace(). But JavaSript also provides methods such as exec(), search(), matchAll(), replaceAll(), and split() that you should be aware of.

While some of these methods belong to the RegExp object, others are properties of the String object. Knowing the difference between these tools and when to use each enables you to write programs that are more compact and more efficient.

test()

The test() method returns a Boolean indicating whether or not a pattern exists in the given string. For example, the following pattern checks if the string contains the substring "day":

```
appendix/methods/methods_ex8.js
const str = "12 days";
const re = /day/;

console.log(re.test(str));     // → true
```

Some regular expression methods such as test() and exec() use the value of lastIndex as the starting position to begin searching the string. If the match succeeds, test() returns true and updates the lastIndex property of the regular expression object. Here's an example:

```
appendix/methods/methods_ex9.js
const str = "10, 20, 30";
const re = /\d\d/g;     // Match two consecutive digits

console.log(re.test(str));      // → true
console.log(re.lastIndex);      // → 2
```

```
console.log(re.test(str));    // → true
console.log(re.lastIndex);    // → 6

// lastIndex is writable
// so you can set it manually
re.lastIndex = 11;
console.log(re.test(str));    // → false
console.log(re.lastIndex);    // → 0
```

Notice Line 13 where test() returns false when it cannot find a match at index 11. When this happens, the method resets lastIndex to 0. Keep in mind that the global flag (g) must be set for this to work.

exec()

The exec() method executes a search on a string. If it finds a match, it returns an array containing the search result. If not, it returns null. Here is an example:

```
appendix/methods/methods_ex1.js
const str = "About 100ft";
const re = /(\d+)ft/;

console.log(re.exec(str));
// → ["100ft", "100", index: 6, input: "About 100ft", groups: undefined]
```

The resulting array contains the matched string as the first item. If there are any capturing groups within the match, they are listed from index 1. The array also comes with three properties:

- index provides the index of the match
- input gets you the original string
- groups lists named capturing groups (if there are any)

If you use a global flag, exec() will use the value of lastIndex as the starting position to begin searching the string. With each call to exec(), the lastIndex property gets changed to reflect the position that follows the last character in the match. Let's look at an example:

```
appendix/methods/methods_ex2.js
const str = "8, 9, 10, 11";
const re = /\d\d/g;

console.log(re.lastIndex);
// → 0

console.log(re.exec(str));
// → ["10", index: 6, input: "8, 9, 10, 11", groups: undefined]
```

```
console.log(re.lastIndex);
// → 8
```

```
console.log(re.exec(str));
// → ["11", index: 10, input: "8, 9, 10, 11", groups: undefined]
```

```
console.log(re.lastIndex);
// → 12
```

```
console.log(re.exec(str));
// → null
```

```
console.log(re.lastIndex);
// → 0
```

In this code, we call exec() multiple times to find successive matches in the same string. When the method cannot find more matches, it returns null and resets the value of lastIndex to 0.

We can also manually modify the value of lastIndex to change the starting position of exec(). For example, let's say we have a numbered list like this:

1. 123
2. 4355
3. 764989

And we want to write a regex to retrieve the value of each item. With lastIndex, we can perform the search only at the position where the data we want is located and greatly simplify the regex pattern:

appendix/methods/methods_ex3.js
```
const str =
`1. 123
2. 4355
3. 764989`;

const re = /\d+/g;

// Split the string into lines
const arr = str.split("\n");

// Loop over the lines and apply regex
arr.forEach(line => {
  re.lastIndex = 2;
  console.log(re.exec(line)[0]);
});

// → 123
// → 4355
// → 764989
```

Two Separate Families

test() and exec() are properties of the RegEx object, so you should call them as a method of a regular expression. Conversely, match(), matchAll(), replace(), replaceAll(), split(), and search() are properties of the String object, and you should call them on a string.

match()

The match() method returns an array similar to exec(). You may have already noticed the similarity between these two methods. Consider this example:

```
appendix/methods/methods_ex4.js
const str = "About 100ft";
const re = /(\d+)ft/;

console.log(str.match(re));
// → ["100ft", "100", index: 6, input: "About 100ft", groups: undefined]

console.log(re.exec(str));
// → ["100ft", "100", index: 6, input: "About 100ft", groups: undefined]
```

exec() and match() return the same result. The output differs only when you set the global flag (g):

```
appendix/methods/methods_ex5.js
const str = "9ft, 10ft, 11ft";
const re = /(\d\d)ft/g;

console.log(str.match(re));
// → ["10ft", "11ft"]

console.log(re.exec(str));
// → ["10ft", "10", index: 5, input: "9ft, 10ft, 11ft", groups: undefined]
```

With the global flag, match() returns an array containing the matched substrings only and won't include capturing groups, indices, and other properties.

Keep in mind that, by default, match() ignores the value you set for lastIndex. To be able to specify the starting position of a search, you have to use the sticky flag (see Recipe 44, Searching from a Specific Index with the y Flag, on page 119).

matchAll()

The matchAll() method is similar to match() except when you set the global flag (g), which causes the method to provide additional information about the matches such as capturing groups and index positions:

```
appendix/methods/methods_ex6.js
const str = "9ft, 10ft, 11ft";
const re = /(\d\d)ft/g;

console.log(str.match(re));
// → ["10ft", "11ft"]

console.log(...str.matchAll(re));
// → ["10ft", "10", index: 5, input: "9ft, 10ft, 11ft", groups: undefined]
// → ["11ft", "11", index: 11, input: "9ft, 10ft, 11ft", groups: undefined]

console.log(re.exec(str));
// → ["10ft", "10", index: 5, input: "9ft, 10ft, 11ft", groups: undefined]
```

matchAll() is a relatively new addition to ECMAScript compared to other methods covered in this appendix. Edge 79 (Released 2020-01-15) was the last browser to implement matchAll().[1] If you need to support older browsers, you can use a polyfill.[2] Previously, developers had to call exec() in a loop to get a similar result, which wasn't very efficient. Here's an example in case you encounter it on the internet:

```
appendix/methods/methods_ex7.js
const str = "9ft, 10ft, 11ft";
const re = /(\d\d)ft/g;

let matches;

while ((matches = re.exec(str)) !== null) {
  console.log(matches);
}

// Logs:
// → ["10ft", "10", index: 5, input: "9ft, 10ft, 11ft", groups: undefined]
// → ["11ft", "11", index: 11, input: "9ft, 10ft, 11ft", groups: undefined]
```

search()

The search() method executes a search on a string and returns an integer indicating the index of the first match. If no match is found, the return value will be -1:

```
appendix/methods/methods_ex10.js
const str = "Eat well, stay fit, die anyway.";

// Using a string as the pattern
console.log(str.search("fit"));    // → 15

// Using a regular expression as the pattern
console.log(str.search(/fit/));    // → 15
```

---

1. https://caniuse.com/mdn-javascript_builtins_string_matchall
2. https://www.npmjs.com/package/string.prototype.matchall

Unlike exec() or test(), the search() method does not support the global flag and ignores the lastIndex property. This means it always executes a search from the beginning of the string and returns the index of the first match.

replace()

The replace() method replaces matches with the given string. The pattern may be a string or a regex:

```
appendix/methods/methods_ex11.js
const str = "fish and chips";

// Using a string as the argument
console.log(str.replace("and", "&"));    // → fish & chips

// Using a regex as the argument
console.log(str.replace(/and/, "&"));    // → fish & chips
```

If the global flag is set, the method replaces every match it finds in the string:

```
appendix/methods/methods_ex12.js
const str = "$5, $10, $20";
const re = /\$/g;

console.log(str.replace(re, "€"));    // → €5, €10, €20
```

replaceAll()

The replaceAll() method outputs the same result as replace() when the global flag is set. Compare:

```
appendix/methods/methods_ex13.js
const str = "$5, $10, $20";
const re = /\$/g;

console.log(str.replace(re, "€"));       // → €5, €10, €20
console.log(str.replaceAll(re, "€"));    // → €5, €10, €20
```

As a result, calling replaceAll() doesn't seem to yield much benefit over calling replace(). The main difference between the two methods is how replaceAll() handles replacement when the pattern is a string, as opposed to a regex:

```
appendix/methods/methods_ex14.js
const str = "$5, $10, $20";
const searchStr = "$";

console.log(str.replace(searchStr, "€"));       // → €5, $10, $20
console.log(str.replaceAll(searchStr, "€"));    // → €5, €10, €20
```

While replaceAll() replaces all instances of a substring, replace() stops searching as soon as it replaces the first substring. Keep in mind that replaceAll() always expects the global flags to be present in a regex pattern; otherwise, it throws an error:

```
appendix/methods/methods_ex15.js
const str = "$5, $10, $20";
const re = /\$/;

str.replaceAll(re, "€");
// → TypeError: String.prototype.replaceAll called with a non-global RegExp
// argument
```

Special Replacement Patterns

The second parameter of replace() and replaceAll() supports a set of special patterns that let you reference different parts of the matched substring. See Recipe 34, Using Special Replacement Patterns, on page 91.

---

split()

The split() method splits a string into substrings and returns them as an array. The first argument, which can be either a string or a regex, specifies the position at which the split should occur. The second argument limits the number of elements returned in the array. Here's an example:

```
appendix/methods/methods_ex16.js
const str = "a b c";

console.log(str.split(" "));       // → ["a", "b", "c"]
console.log(str.split(/\s/, 2));   // → ["a", "b"]
```

Indices

If you set the d flag in a regex, you'll have access to the indices property in the result of exec(), match(), and matchAll(). For more on indices, see Recipe 40, Generating Indices for Matches with the d Flag, on page 107.

Conclusion

In summary, use...

- test() when you want to check whether a pattern exists in a string

- search() when you want to get the index of a match

- match() or exec() when you want to get all information about a match

- exec() when you want to use lastIndex as the starting position to begin searching

- match() with the global flag when you want to obtain all matches but don't care about other properties

- matchAll() when you want to obtain all information about all matches

- replace() when you want to replace one or all instances of a string/regex pattern

- replaceAll() when you want to replace all instances of a string/regex pattern

- split() when you want to split a string into an array of substrings

Testing Regex with Specialized Tools

Deciphering complex regular expression patterns can be difficult even for experienced developers. As a result, many regular expression tools (both free and commercial) have emerged with varying feature sets that make building regex patterns easier.

While it's perfectly possible to experiment with regular expressions in a programming environment, you'd be missing useful helpers such as syntax checking, debugging, and other feedback.

A good tool provides an interface to test a pattern on sample strings, makes it easier to understand complex regular expressions written by other developers, and allows you to convert regular expressions between flavors.

When building complicated regular expressions, using a specialized tool like the ones described below will make your code less prone to errors.

RegexPal

RegexPal is a simple web-based regular expression tester written entirely in JavaScript.

To test a regular expression using RegexPal, open regexpal.com in your browser and type a pattern in the box at the top. In the bottom box, enter the target text you want to match.

You will see that RegexPal automatically highlights the portion of the text that matches your regex. The program also indicates any syntax errors in your pattern. A nice feature of RegexPal is the ability to provide information as you type without the need to click on a button to see the result, making it very convenient to use.

https://regexpal.com

RegExr

RegExr is a feature-packed tool to build regular expressions with real-time updates as you type.

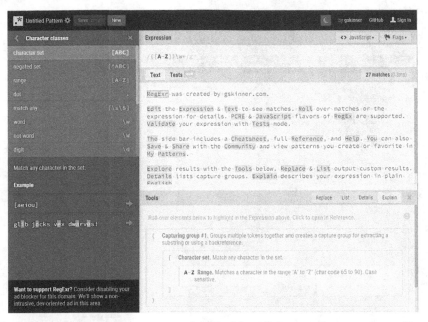

RegExr's Explain tool gives you a detailed breakdown of your regex. You can mouse over the regex tokens to see a description of what each of them does. An interesting feature of RegExr is the ability to save a regular expression to a short link, allowing you to share patterns with others easily.

Other features include syntax highlighting, contextual help, cheat sheets, references, searchable community patterns, and more. RegExr supports JavaScript and PHP/PCRE flavors.

https://regexr.com

Regex101

Regex101 is a popular web-based regular expression tester that supports multiple flavors, including JavaScript, Python, PCRE, Java, .NET(C#) and Golang.

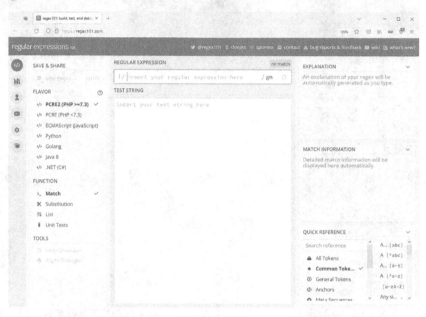

Regex101 provides a debugger with a real-time explanation that shows every step the engine takes. It can detect errors, highlight the syntax, show the capturing groups, allow substitutions, and provide a detailed explanation of each token.

Similar to RegExr, Regex101 has the ability to permanently save a regular expression to a short link and share your pattern with others.

https://regex101.com

RegexBuddy

RegexBuddy is a powerful tool for the Windows operating system that provides an interface for creating, testing, and debugging regular expressions.

RegexBuddy offers regex analysis to quickly understand a pattern and automatically highlights the syntax as you edit. A helpful feature of RegexBuddy is the ability to compare a regex between multiple flavors to ensure it works as intended across platforms and programming languages.

It also incorporates a tool for converting regular expressions between flavors. Additionally, RegexBuddy comes with a library of patterns to solve various text-matching problems quickly. For example, there are ready-to-use patterns for matching dates, domain names, national IDs of different countries, etc.

RegexBuddy supports all of the popular regex flavors, including JavaScript.

https://www.regexbuddy.com

Regex Vis

Regex Vis is a diagramming application that lets you create a concise visual representation of regex structures:

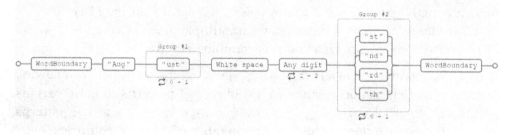

Railroad diagrams can be a helpful aid in comprehending complex regex patterns. Type your pattern into the provided box, and the app will generate a corresponding diagram immediately. For example, if you enter the regex /\bAug(ust)?\s\d{1,2}(st|nd|rd|th)?\b/ from Recipe 30, Regex Vis will create the following diagram:

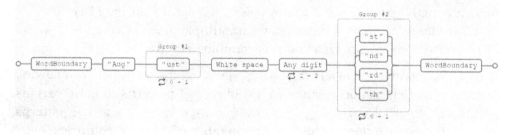

https://regex-vis.com/

Regular Expression Cheat Sheet

Regular expressions can be complex and difficult to remember. That's where a cheat sheet comes in handy. This quick reference guide provides a summary of the regex syntax in JavaScript and its meanings, making it easy to find and use the right pattern for your needs.

Character Classes

Syntax	Description
.	Matches any character except newline.
\w	Matches any word character (letter, digit, or underscore).
\W	Matches any non-word character.
\d	Matches any digit character.
\D	Matches any non-digit character.
\s	Matches any whitespace character.
\S	Matches any non-whitespace character.
[abc]	Matches any of the characters inside the brackets.
[^abc]	Matches any character not inside the brackets.
[a-z]	Matches any character between a and z (inclusive).

Quantifiers

Syntax	Description
x*	Matches zero or more occurrences of the preceding character.
x+	Matches one or more occurrences of the preceding character.
x?	Matches zero or one occurrence of the preceding character.
x{n}	Matches exactly n occurrences of the preceding character.
x{n,}	Matches at least n occurrences of the preceding character.
x{n,m}	Matches between n and m occurrences of the preceding character (inclusive).
x*?	Lazy quantifier: matches the shortest possible sequence of characters
x+?	in a string that satisfies a given pattern.
x??	
x{n}?	
x{n,}?	
x{n,m}?	

Boundary Assertions

Syntax	Description
^	Matches the beginning of a string.
$	Matches the end of a string.
\b	Matches a word boundary.
\B	Matches a non-word boundary.

Lookaround Assertions

Syntax	Lookaround Type	Description
x(?=y)	Positive Lookahead	Matches "x" only if followed by "y."
x(?!y)	Negative Lookahead	Matches "x" only if not followed by "y."
(?<=y)x	Positive Lookbehind	Matches "x" only if preceded by "y."
(?<!y)x	Negative Lookbehind	Matches "x" only if not preceded by "y."

Groups and Backreferences

Syntax	Group Type	Description
(x)	Capturing Group	Captures the matched substring and assigns it a group number.
(?<Name>x)	Named Capturing Group	Captures the matched substring by name and assigns it a group number.
(?:x)	Non-Capturing Group	Matches "x" but does not capture it as a group.
\n	Backreference	Matches the same text as the nth captured group.
k<Name>	Backreference to a Named Capturing Group	Matches the same text as the nth named captured group.

Flags

Syntax	Flag Type	Description
g	global	Finds all matches, not just the first one.
i	ignoreCase	Matches upper and lowercase characters.
s	dotAll	Allows the dot (.) to match newlines.
u	unicode	Enables various Unicode features.
y	sticky	Matches only at the current position in the target string.
d	hasIndices	Enables the result of a match to contain the start and end indices of the substrings.
m	multiline	Matches the beginning or end of each line in a string, not just the beginning or end of the string itself.

Unicode Property Escapes

Syntax	Type	Description
\p{UnicodePropertyValue}	Positive Unicode Property Escape	Matches characters based on their Unicode properties.
\P{UnicodePropertyValue}	Negative Unicode Property Escape	Matches any character that does not have the specified Unicode property value.

Index

Thank you!

We hope you enjoyed this book and that you're already thinking about what you want to learn next. To help make that decision easier, we're offering you this gift.

Head on over to https://pragprog.com right now, and use the coupon code BUYANOTHER2024 to save 30% on your next ebook. Offer is void where prohibited or restricted. This offer does not apply to any edition of the *The Pragmatic Programmer* ebook.

And if you'd like to share your own expertise with the world, why not propose a writing idea to us? After all, many of our best authors started off as our readers, just like you. With up to a 50% royalty, world-class editorial services, and a name you trust, there's nothing to lose. Visit https://pragprog.com/become-an-author/ today to learn more and to get started.

We thank you for your continued support, and we hope to hear from you again soon!

The Pragmatic Bookshelf

Pragmatic Bookshelf

SAVE 30%!
Use coupon code
BUYANOTHER2024

A Common-Sense Guide to Data Structures and Algorithms in Python, Volume 1

If you thought data structures and algorithms were all just theory, you're missing out on what they can do for your Python code. Learn to use Big O notation to make your code run faster by orders of magnitude. Choose from data structures such as hash tables, trees, and graphs to increase your code's efficiency exponentially. With simple language and clear diagrams, this book makes this complex topic accessible, no matter your background. Every chapter features practice exercises to give you the hands-on information you need to master data structures and algorithms for your day-to-day work.

Jay Wengrow
(502 pages) ISBN: 979-8-88865-035-6. $57.95
https://pragprog.com/book/jwpython

Text Processing with Ruby

Whatever you want to do with text, Ruby is up to the job. No matter what the source – web pages, databases, the contents of files – learn how to acquire the text and get it into your program. Explore techniques to process that text and then output the transformed or extracted text. Cut even the most complex text-based tasks down to size and learn how to master regular expressions, scrape information from Web pages, develop reusable utilities to process text in pipelines, and more.

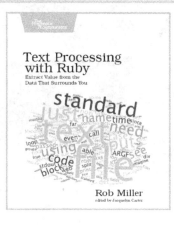

Rob Miller
(272 pages) ISBN: 9781680500707. $36
https://pragprog.com/book/rmtpruby

Designing Data Governance from the Ground Up

Businesses own more data than ever before, but it's of no value if you don't know how to use it. Data governance manages the people, processes, and strategy needed for deploying data projects to production. But doing it well is far from easy: Less than one fourth of business leaders say their organizations are data driven. In *Designing Data Governance from the Ground Up*, you'll build a cross-functional strategy to create roadmaps and stewardship for data-focused projects, embed data governance into your engineering practice, and put processes in place to monitor data after deployment.

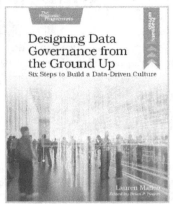

Lauren Maffeo
(100 pages) ISBN: 9781680509809. $29.95
https://pragprog.com/book/lmmlops

From Objects to Functions

Build applications quicker and with less effort using functional programming and Kotlin. Learn by building a complete application, from gathering requirements to delivering a microservice architecture following functional programming principles. Learn how to implement CQRS and EventSourcing in a functional way to map the domain into code better and to keep the cost of change low for the whole application life cycle.

If you're curious about functional programming or you are struggling with how to put it into practice, this guide will help you increase your productivity composing small functions together instead of creating fat objects.

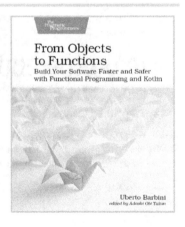

Uberto Barbini
(468 pages) ISBN: 9781680508451. $47.95
https://pragprog.com/book/uboop

The Pragmatic Bookshelf

The Pragmatic Bookshelf features books written by professional developers for professional developers. The titles continue the well-known Pragmatic Programmer style and continue to garner awards and rave reviews. As development gets more and more difficult, the Pragmatic Programmers will be there with more titles and products to help you stay on top of your game.

Visit Us Online

This Book's Home Page
https://pragprog.com/book/fkjavascript
Source code from this book, errata, and other resources. Come give us feedback, too!

Keep Up-to-Date
https://pragprog.com
Join our announcement mailing list (low volume) or follow us on Twitter @pragprog for new titles, sales, coupons, hot tips, and more.

New and Noteworthy
https://pragprog.com/news
Check out the latest Pragmatic developments, new titles, and other offerings.

Save on the ebook

Save on the ebook versions of this title. Owning the paper version of this book entitles you to purchase the electronic versions at a terrific discount.

PDFs are great for carrying around on your laptop—they are hyperlinked, have color, and are fully searchable. Most titles are also available for the iPhone and iPod touch, Amazon Kindle, and other popular e-book readers.

Send a copy of your receipt to support@pragprog.com and we'll provide you with a discount coupon.

Contact Us

Online Orders:	*https://pragprog.com/catalog*
Customer Service:	*support@pragprog.com*
International Rights:	*translations@pragprog.com*
Academic Use:	*academic@pragprog.com*
Write for Us:	*http://write-for-us.pragprog.com*

Printed in the USA
CPSIA information can be obtained
at www.ICGtesting.com
JSHW062150050224
56676JS00012B/178